ACKNOWLEDGMENTS

The U.S. Department of Transportation (USDOT) Volpe National Transportation Systems Center (Volpe Center), in coordination with the U.S. Fish and Wildlife Service (USFWS), prepared this study, which was funded in 2007 by the Federal Transit Administration Alternative Transportation in Parks and Public Lands (ATPPL) program, now called the Paul S. Sarbanes Transit in the Parks Program (TRIP). The project team included Anna Biton, Theresa Perrone and Julianne Schwarzer of the Volpe Center's Transportation Policy, Planning, and Organizational Excellence Division.

The authors wish to thank the numerous organizations and individuals who graciously provided their time, knowledge and guidance in the development of this report. Those of particular note are listed below:

Carl Melberg, Refuge Planner (U.S. Fish and Wildlife Service, Eastern Massachusetts NWR Complex)
Libby Herland, Project Leader (U.S. Fish and Wildlife Service, Eastern Massachusetts NWR Complex)
Michel Brady (U.S. Fish and Wildlife Service)
John C. Sauer (U.S. Fish and Wildlife Service)

Terry Whalen (Town of Chatham, Department of Community Development)
Clay Schofield (Cape Cod Commission)

Jeff Colby (Town of Chatham, Department of Public Works)
Lisa Franz (Chatham Chamber of Commerce)

TABLE OF CONTENTS

List of Maps

List of Tables

EXECUTIVE SUMMARY

The purpose of the Monomoy National Wildlife Refuge (MNWR) Alternative Transportation Study is to explore potential alternative transportation options that can address a variety of transportation safety and access issues. MNWR consists of a visitor contact station, refuge headquarters and trails on Morris Island (connected to the mainland by a causeway), South Monomoy (connected to the mainland) and the North Monomoy Island (accessible only by boat). The MNWR visitor contact station is open daily during the summer months and intermittently during the offseason. Two private ferry services operate 25-passenger boats and are permitted to bring visitors to the Monomoy. Visitors to Morris Island and ferry passengers use the limited parking lot at the MNWR headquarters/visitor contact station.

The majority of the land on Morris Island is privately owned, and access to the headquarters/visitor contact station is provided via a right of way over private land. There have been some disputes between FWS and neighboring land owners over levels of visitation and traffic, and some encroachment on the right-of-way itself.

While there is regional public transportation service to Chatham, the closest stops are located more than two miles from MNWR. Access to the refuge is primarily by private automobile; the access roads are narrow and lack bicycle and pedestrian facilities, and the refuge is not located in close proximity to other destinations. The causeway leading to Morris Island has two narrow travel lanes and no shoulder; parking allowed on one side of the roadway effectively reduces the roadway to 1.5 lanes. This creates potential safety hazards to motorists, pedestrians and cyclists, and presents challenges to emergency responders needing to access Morris Island in case of emergency. There is limited directional or informational signage available to assist visitors to MNWR. Many visitors get lost on their way to the refuge, sometimes venturing onto private property or deciding not to try to visit after all.

While many of these issues are not currently operating at "crisis levels," there are real access and safety concerns, which FWS wants to address proactively in order to prevent aggravating them in the future.

Existing Conditions
Monomoy National Wildlife Refuge (MNWR) is located in the Cape Cod town of Chatham, Massachusetts, just over 90 miles from Boston, Massachusetts. Sitting on the southeastern shore of the Cape, Chatham is a favorite summer vacationing spot for many New England residents and is home to 6,625 full time residents.[1] The town's harbors are home to both recreational boats and commercial fishing fleets. Although only 16.2 square miles, Chatham is surrounded by water on 3 sides and has more than 1,000 acres of public oceanside and bayside and beaches, not including MNWR.

---

[1] Data Table (sf3, pop), 2000 US Census

Environmental protection and preservation is a high priority in Chatham. Thus, recommendations of this study must be consistent with this priority in order to be politically viable. The tourism industry is also of vital importance to the Chatham community, as the local economy is driven by visitors and summer residents. Unfortunately, tourism patterns lead to traffic congestion and other transportation challenges during the high season in Chatham. If no measures are taken to alleviate congestion and safety concerns, the transportation challenges in Chatham could worsen. This study begins with the knowledge that existing development patterns and community preservation priorities limit opportunities for roadway widening, building new parking facilities, and the use of full-size transit vehicles.

Project Goals

The primary goal of the MNWR Alternative Transportation Study is to identify transportation intervention options that could improve alternative transportation access to MNWR. While this study focuses primarily on MNWR, it takes into account important relationships to transportation within Chatham as a whole, particularly related to the downtown area and access to the federally owned Lighthouse Beach. The study identifies interventions that: improve multi-modal access to MNWR and within Chatham, reduce traffic and parking congestion around MNWR and within Chatham, improve traveler safety, enhance the visitor experience and develop and enhance partnerships with governmental and non-governmental agencies.

Methodology

This study includes chapters on stakeholder involvement, partnerships, transportation interventions and alternative transportation scenarios. Data collection, evaluation and analysis were conducted separately for each section.

As part of stakeholder involvement, the study team gathered information pertaining to transportation alternatives from stakeholders in the study area, including year-round and seasonal Chatham residents, the local business community, elected officials, town and regional planning staff, and others. There were multiple opportunities for stakeholders to identify high-priority transportation concerns and potential solutions.

In the partnership assessment, the study team developed a broad list of existing local government departments, civic groups, and organizations in the greater Chatham area. Then, the study team and MNWR staff discussed the current partnership conditions, outlined ways to strengthen or expand upon existing partnerships and identified potential new partners. The study team gathered additional information about potential partners from existing reports, web sites, other literature and brief interviews. These findings were used to identify possible activities for each partnership, including initiatives and projects that could be implemented by MNWR and those that could be implemented by the partner. The discussion of potential alternative transportation scenarios identifies the key partnerships necessary to ensure the success of each suggested transportation intervention.

In order to develop alternative transportation scenarios, the team first brainstormed and identified 39 potential interventions to address local transportation issues and meet project goals. Each intervention was evaluated based on a set of 10 criteria related to its feasibility and impact. Based on this assessment, 21 interventions were researched in greater detail to understand how MNWR could implement these interventions.

The interventions were used to develop four scenarios, by combining several interventions, to meet multiple project goals. The scenarios are intended to provide various examples of how alternative transportation access improvements could be approached, with some scenarios requiring more technically complicated interventions than others. There is a wide range of costs and time required to implement each of the four scenarios, in order to provide multiple options for FWS to consider in planning for the future. For each scenario, the project team considered whether the suite of interventions was likely to achieve the goal, could possibly achieve the goal, was unlikely to achieve the goal, or was not applicable. The assessments are qualitative, and meant to describe the potential implications of implementing a given scenario.

Findings and Conclusions

The MNWR Alternative Transportation Study provides a wide range of information and potential transportation-related interventions that FWS could pursue to improve access to and information about MNWR. While this study does not make specific recommendations for what FWS should implement, it provides FWS with the tools to make informed decisions on how to meet its goals through pursuing alternative transportation improvements. In addition, the study identifies partners whose participation in an alternative transportation intervention increase the potential for success.

The information in this study will provide important background information for FWS as it moves forward to develop the Comprehensive Conservation Plan (CCP) for the Monomoy National Wildlife Refuge.

1. PURPOSE AND BACKGROUND

The U.S. Fish and Wildlife Service (FWS) Monomoy National Wildlife Refuge (MNWR) is located in the town of Chatham, Massachusetts. In addition to the refuge, Chatham boasts small-town charm and many seaside amenities, making it popular for both residents and visitors. Access to the refuge is very limited without use of a personal automobile, which adds to the already high levels of seasonal traffic congestion that the town experiences, due in part to narrow roadways, limited parking, and limited transit service.

In 2007 the FWS submitted an application for funding from the Federal Transit Administration (FTA) Alternative Transportation in Parks and Public Lands (ATPPL) program, now called the Paul S. Sarbanes Transit in the Parks Program (TRIP), to study alternative transportation options to improve access to MNWR and within the Chatham area, as well as to Lighthouse Beach, which is located within the Cape Cod National Seashore and managed by the town of Chatham.

An interagency Transportation Assistance Group (TAG) conducted a field investigation of the transportation infrastructure and issues at MNWR on July 17-19, 2007, on behalf of FWS. The TAG team report, prepared subsequent to the site visit, documented the conditions observed, transportation issues and considerations, and recommendations for moving forward.

Following the TAG report, FWS selected the U.S. Department of Transportation Volpe National Transportation Systems Center (Volpe Center) to conduct the Monomoy National Wildlife Refuge Alternative Transportation Study. The study examines existing transportation conditions, presents and evaluates several alternative transportation options, assesses partnership opportunities, and provides implementation considerations for alternatives. The research process marries data collection and analysis with input from the public – including full-time and seasonal residents, the business community, and other stakeholders.

FWS has also begun to develop the fifteen-year Comprehensive Conservation Plan (CCP) for MNWR. The CCP is the primary management document for the refuge; FWS will consider implementation of transportation-related activities identified in this study as part of the CCP process.

1.1. Purpose and Problem Statement

The purpose of this study is to explore potential alternative transportation interventions that can address a variety of transportation safety and access issues. MNWR consists of a visitor contact station, refuge headquarters and trails on Morris Island (connected to the mainland by a causeway), South Monomoy (connected to the mainland) and the North Monomoy Island (accessible only by boat). The MNWR visitor contact station is open daily during the summer months and intermittently during the offseason. Two private ferry services operate 25-passenger boats and are permitted to bring visitors to the Monomoy islands.

Passengers on one of the ferry services and other visitors to Morris Island use the parking lot located at the MNWR headquarters/visitor contact station.

The majority of the land on Morris Island is privately owned, and access to the headquarters/visitor contact station is provided via a right of way over private land. There have been disputes between FWS and neighboring land owners over levels of visitation and traffic, as well as neighbor encroachment on the right-of-way itself.

While there is regional public transportation service to Chatham, the closest stops are located over two miles away from MNWR. Access is primarily by private automobile; the access roads are narrow and lack bicycle and pedestrian facilities, and the refuge is not located in close proximity to other destinations. The causeway leading to Morris Island has two narrow travel lanes and no shoulder; parking allowed on one side of the roadway effectively reduces the roadway to 1.5 lanes. This creates potential safety hazards to motorists, pedestrians and cyclists, and presents challenges to emergency responders needing to access Morris Island in case of emergency.

Finally, there is limited directional or informational signage to guide visitors to MNWR. Many visitors get lost en route to the refuge, sometimes venturing onto private property or deciding to forego the visit.

While many of these issues are not currently operating at "crisis levels," there are real access and safety concerns, which FWS wants to address proactively in order to prevent aggravating them in the future.

1.2. Project Goals

The primary goal of the MNWR Alternative Transportation Study is to identify options for improving alternative transportation access to MNWR. While this study focuses primarily on MNWR, it takes into account important relationships to transportation within Chatham as a whole, particularly related to the downtown area and access to the town-managed Lighthouse Beach, which is located within the Cape Cod National Seashore. Within this umbrella are goals related to access, traffic and parking, safety, visitor experience and partnerships. Examples of these goals are presented below.

- Improve multi-modal access to MNWR and within Chatham
    - Improve pedestrian/bicycle access to MNWR
    - Provide transit service to MNWR
    - Promote MNWR access via alternate transportation modes
    - Provide connections to regional transit service
    - Provide access improvements during peak summer season
    - Improve water access options to Monomoy Islands
    - Utilize neighborhood scale systems to address transportation needs

- Reduce traffic and parking congestion around MNWR and within Chatham

- o   Reduce traffic congestion in downtown Chatham
- o   Reduce traffic congestion to Morris Island
- o   Reduce parking pressure at MNWR Headquarters
- o   Utilize existing paved areas for alternate parking opportunities to serve MNWR visitors

- Improve traveler safety
  - o   Improve safety on Causeway
  - o   Improve safety on Bridge St.
  - o   Improve bicycle and pedestrian safety

- Enhance visitor experience
  - o   Eliminate/reduce visitor confusion and travel through private neighborhoods
  - o   Improve visitor awareness/information about MNWR

- Develop and enhance partnerships with governmental and non-governmental agencies
  - o   Maintain/develop partnerships between the refuge and municipal and regional entities
  - o   Consider and ensure consistency with town goals, such as:
    - ▪   Protect against increased dominance of automobile
    - ▪   Protect character of neighborhood centers
    - ▪   Promote safety of bicyclists and pedestrians
    - ▪   Protect sensitive environmental resources
  - o   Maintain economic and social benefits from tourism

2. EXISTING CONDITIONS

2.1. Location and Context

Monomoy National Wildlife Refuge (MNWR) is located in the Cape Cod town of Chatham, Massachusetts, just over 90 miles from Boston, Massachusetts. Sitting on the southeastern shore of the Cape, Chatham is a favorite summer vacationing spot for many New England residents and is home to 6,625 full time residents.[2] The town's harbors are home to both recreational boats and commercial fishing fleets. Although only 16.2 square miles, Chatham is surrounded by water on 3 sides and has more than 1,000 acres of public oceanside and bayside beaches, not including MNWR.

Map 1: Cape Cod and Chatham

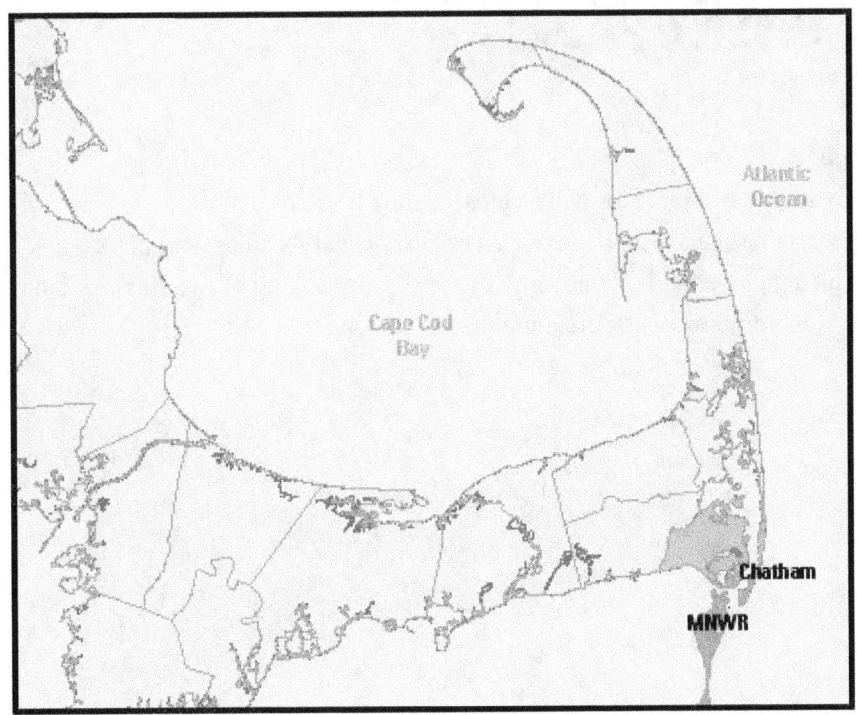

Source: MassGIS

Part-time residents and tourists are drawn to Chatham's traditional village center, small-scale business district and its natural beauty. The town is home to three lighthouses – the Chatham Lighthouse, the Stage Harbor Lighthouse, and the Monomoy Lighthouse. All are popular areas for scenic views. Lighthouse Beach is one of

---

[2] Data Table (sf3, pop), 2000 US Census

the Chatham's most popular beaches and is the southernmost extremity of the Cape Cod National Seashore. While technically on Federal land, the Town of Chatham manages the beach.

Key Sites

Lighthouse Beach

Monomoy National Wildlife Refuge

Monomoy is an eight mile sandy stretch that includes two islands extending southwest off of the coast of Chatham. The 7,604 acre refuge, established in 1944, provides a critical habitat for migratory birds, most notable the federally-protected piping plover and roseate tern. The refuge is made up of two barrier islands, North Monomoy Island, South Monomoy, and a 40 acre unit on Morris Island.

Map 2: Monomoy National Wildlife Refuge

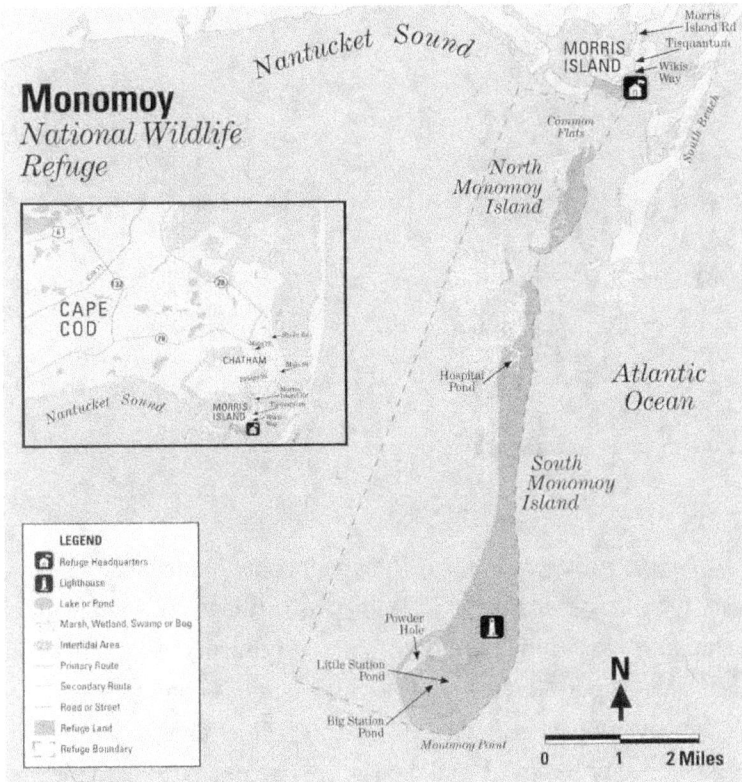

Source: U.S. FWS

The Morris Island section of Monomoy houses the refuge headquarters and visitor contact station and is the only section of the refuge that is accessible by land. The barrier islands, known as North Monomoy Island (2.5 miles long) and South Monomoy (5 miles long), are accessible only by boat.

The Monomoy Islands constantly change in size and shape due to erosion and sand drifts from the outer beaches. The islands, left when glaciers retreated, are estimated to be roughly 6,000 years old. By the 20th century, Monomoy grew from a group of small islands to an arm of land connected to Cape Cod. In 1958, a storm divided much of Monomoy from the shore and twenty years later the North and South Monomoy Islands were split from each other by a blizzard.

MNWR Entrance

The Monomoy area was originally inhabited by Native Americans. It was first mapped by English and French explorers in the 16th century. By the 19th century the small town known as Whitewash Village grew along the southern end of Monomoy and operated as a shipping and fishing port for 30 years. Eventually, sand drifts closed the inlet that made Whitewash Village a valuable port, forcing boats to other ports. A community persisted in Whitewash Village into the 1930s, however most residents were seasonal. Over time, the Whitewash Village's summer cottages were abandoned or removed, and the last cottage remained until the spring of 2000.

Cape Cod

Cape Cod, the world's largest glacial peninsula, is largely composed of materials deposited by retreating glaciers approximately 15,000 years ago. The resulting dynamic landform consists of windswept beaches and forested uplands, sheer bluffs and rolling dunes, freshwater ponds and saltwater marshes. Since its formation, Cape Cod's coastline has experienced significant physical change, a result of inevitable coastal processes shaped by winds, waves, tides and currents. In addition to these erosive forces, a few areas are also experiencing accretion, or the gradual buildup of land caused by the steady deposition of sand and sediment by ocean currents. Thus, both erosion and accretion are taking place at several beach sites in these areas.

Sea-level rise and global climate change are related issues that will likely impact the Cape's low-lying areas, but the relative rise in sea level will depend on subsidence (the downward movement of the Earth's surface) and other coastal processes. Scientists do not yet know the impact that climate change will have on storm frequency or severity, or the threats to the Cape's developed areas and its transportation network.

Quitnesset

While there are no remaining cottages from Whitewash Village in Monomoy itself, the close knit and affluent neighborhood of Quitnesset is adjacent to MNWR. Access to the refuge is provided by a right of way crossing several privately-owned parcels in Quitnesset.

While the neighbors enjoy the resources and quiet provided by the refuge, there are concerns about access to the federal property located almost literally "in their backyards." A neighborhood association is engaged in dialogue with refuge management about the relationship between refuge visitation and traffic congestion. While the FWS mission focuses on habitat protection, improving access for visitors in a sustainable and sensitive way is a valuable goal. The Improvement Act of 1997 requires FWS to allow compatible public uses on refuges.

Refuge Management and Visitation

MNWR is part of the U.S. Fish and Wildlife Service (USFWS) National Wildlife Refuge System. Its mission is to "administer a national network of lands and waters for the conservation, management, and where appropriate, restoration of the fish, wildlife, and plant resources and their habitats within the U.S. for the benefit of present and future generations of Americans." The refuge system is made up of more than 150 million acres of land on more than 550 wildlife refuges. Maintaining biological integrity, diversity and environmental health of refuge lands is important, as is providing opportunities for the public to engage in compatible, wildlife-dependent public use. These uses are hunting, fishing, wildlife observation, wildlife photography, environmental education, and interpretation. At MNWR, all of these uses except hunting are provided.[3]

MNWR Headquarters/Visitor contact station

---

[3] U.S. Fish and Wildlife Service National Refuge System Website, U.S. Fish and Wildlife Service

In addition to its protective status as a national wildlife refuge, Monomoy is also part of the National Wilderness Preservation System, with most of the refuge protected by this designation since 1970. MNWR is a staffed satellite of the Eastern Massachusetts NWR Complex, which is headquartered in Sudbury, MA. The MNWR headquarters/visitor contact station houses 4 year-round employees as well as seasonal staff, interns and volunteers. The headquarters/visitor contact station is generally open Monday through Friday, and in the summer is open on Saturdays as well. The building is closed when staff or volunteers are not available to greet the public.

The visitor contact station is a resource for refuge information, maps, and environmental education. Many visitors do not stop in the contact station, and instead access the refuge on their own or through a local tourism company. Most visitors who use the contact station pass through the refuge in the late morning through the early afternoon during the summer season, between Memorial Day and Labor Day. While roughly 20,000 visitors pass through the Monomoy visitor contact station each year, approximately 50,000 visitors use the refuge parking lot during the summer months.[4] Visitors to Monomoy enjoy wildlife observation, seal-watching, and recreational activities. The refuge itself is known worldwide for its bird watching and was designated as a Western Hemispheric Shorebird Reserve Network Site (WHSRN) and an Important Bird Area Site (IBA). The beauty and wilderness of Monomoy draws 50,000 counted annual visitors.

Eastern Massachusetts NWR Complex
MNWR is one of eight refuges that make up the Eastern Massachusetts NWR Complex. The other refuges in the complex include: Assabet River, Great Meadows, Mashpee, Massasoit, Nantucket, Nomans Land Island, and Oxbow NWRs. The refuge complex is situated along the Atlantic flyway, and each of the ecologically diverse refuges provides critical habitat for migratory birds, plants, and other wildlife.

---

[4] MNWR TAG Report, Inter-Agency TAG Session

Map 3: Eastern Massachusetts National Wildlife Refuge Complex

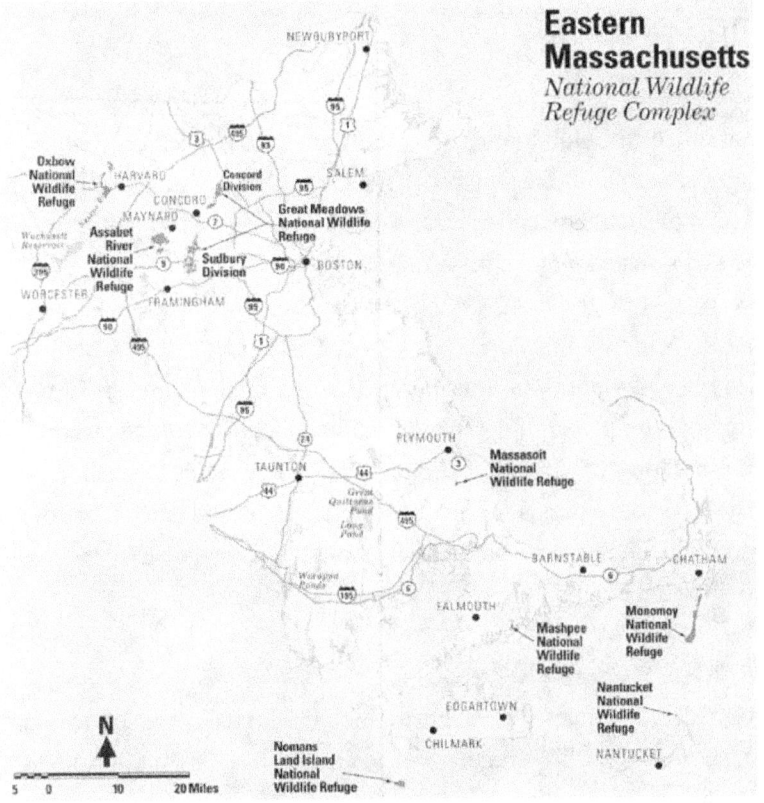

Source: U.S. FWS

The Refuge Complex manages all eight refuges to conserve and protect diversity of native habitats and species. Monomoy provides habitat for the threatened piping plover and endangered roseate tern. This study is the first transportation planning study for a refuge within the Refuge Complex.

Habitat Management

Monomoy creates a "safe harbor" for coastal birds; the refuge is a safe haven for small birds, such as terns, and in 1996 FWS established a "gull free zone" over one portion of South Monomoy. Since that time, the area experienced a rise in federally-protected roseate tern and piping plover populations.

Monomoy is also home to the federally protected Northeastern Beach Tiger Beetle. The use of off-road vehicles and the manipulation of beach habitat caused a decline in the beetle's population; today, Monomoy's beetles are collected as part of a federal management program based on Martha's Vineyard, MA.

2.2. Partners and Stakeholders

There are several entities with a jurisdictional interest in Monomoy and its transportation challenges. The National Park Service (NPS), Cape Cod National Seashore (the Seashore), the Cape Cod Commission (CCC), the Commonwealth of Massachusetts, the Town of Chatham, and the Cape Cod Regional Transit Authority (CCRTA) have relationships with the refuge and a vested interest in its future.

The National Park Service (NPS) and Cape Cod National Seashore
Created in 1961 by President John F. Kennedy, the Seashore was considered an experiment in preservation, overseen by the NPS. Unlike other National Parks comprised of donated or publicly held land, the Seashore was formed as an attempt to conserve the fragile shores of Cape Cod and provide opportunities for visitors to experience and enjoy the natural features. The Seashore extends for nearly 40 miles along the outer shore of Cape Cod. Lighthouse Beach in Chatham is within the Seashore boundaries, though it is managed by the town. Partnerships between NPS, FWS, and the town could result in improved access for visitors.

Cape Cod Regional Transit Authority (CCRTA)
The Cape Cod Regional Transit Authority (CCRTA) operates several buses, including fixed route services and the door to door "B-Bus Service" paratransit service. CCRTA's regular service is low cost, and multi ride passes are available. The regular routes serve the majority of Cape Cod.

The Seashore and the CCRTA partnered to implement two transit services, the Provincetown Shuttle and the FlexRoute (Flex) bus line. The Flex, which began in 2006, serves the Outer Cape towns of Provincetown, Truro, Wellfleet, Eastham, Orleans, Brewster, and Harwich, as well as the Cape Cod National Seashore, and runs Monday through Saturday. It operates primarily along Routes 6 and 6A, and allows passengers to schedule pick-ups and drop-offs within a 0.75-mile distance of the main route. This flexibility allows users of the Seashore more freedom when exploring the Cape Cod coastline.

While Monomoy is not part of the Seashore, it borders a NPS beach, and a flexible transit service could benefit both resources. Flex does not currently serve Chatham, but converting the existing Hyannis-to-Orleans (H2O) line to a Flex-type service has been discussed. The Cape Cod Commission incorporated the potential addition of Flex-like service into Chatham into its planning documents.

Cape Cod Commission (CCC)
The Cape Cod Commission (CCC) is the regional land use and transportation planning agency for the 15 towns that make up Barnstable County (Cape Cod). Created in 1990, the mission of the CCC is to protect Cape Cod's environment and character, assuring a healthy community for both current and future residents and visitors. The CCC transportation staff serves as the lead planning staff for the Cape Cod Metropolitan Planning Organization.

The new CCC Cape Cod Regional Policy Plan took effect on January 29, 2009. The plan outlines guidelines and goals for environment and transportation, both of which could directly impact Monomoy. By working together, Monomoy and the CCC could both achieve their goals and satisfy some of the accessibility issues associated with the Chatham seashore.

Town of Chatham

As the host community, the Town of Chatham is a natural partner with FWS, as a relationship between the two entities is mutually beneficial. Both are in a position to improve accessibility and transportation in the areas of Chatham nearest the refuge.

Chatham operates under a Town Meeting form of government that includes five selectmen and an executive secretary. Citizens meet annually to discuss town articles, then pass or reject them.[5] Peak season parking and traffic issues feature prominently at town meetings.

Other Civic Groups

Chatham is known as a civically-active community with many groups that serve the public interest. The Chatham Chamber of Commerce, the Cape Cod Chamber of Commerce, the Chatham Historical Society, and the Rotary Club are a few of the many civic groups who hold a stake in MNWR.

These civic groups are important stakeholders who can contribute to the dialogue about access, traffic and transportation solutions.

2.3. Land Use, Development, and Demographics

Trends and Patterns in Land Use and Development

Chatham was incorporated in 1712, and the current land use pattern was well established by 1900. The town became a popular summer resort destination in the 1800s, and many people from Boston and New York purchased tracts of land and built large homes. There is a traditional town center east of the Oyster Pond, and neighborhood centers along Route 28. Since 1945, the population of Chatham has more than tripled and residential development has increased greatly. A total of 5,185 housing units were built between 1950 and 2000, with more than half (2,690) built during the 20-year period from 1970 to 1989. Only 1,535 units had been built prior to 1950[6]. Water and ocean cover approximately one-third of the area within Chatham's boundaries. Approximately half of the land area is developed for residential use; approximately half of the houses are seasonal and one third of the adult population is retired. Table 1 shows approximate land usage of the non-water areas.

---

[5] DHCD Chatham Community Profile. Massachusetts Department of Housing and Community Development
6 2000 U.S. Census, SF3

Table 1: Chatham Land Use7

Use	Acres	Percent of Total
Residential	3,819	41%
Open / Recreational	2,026	22%
Forest / Agricultural	1,850	20%
Wetland	1,081	12%
Municipal	188	2%
Commercial	211	2%
Industrial	90	1%
Total	**9,264**	**100%**

Map 4 shows the distribution of land uses within Chatham.

---

[7] MassGIS

Map 4: Chatham Land Uses

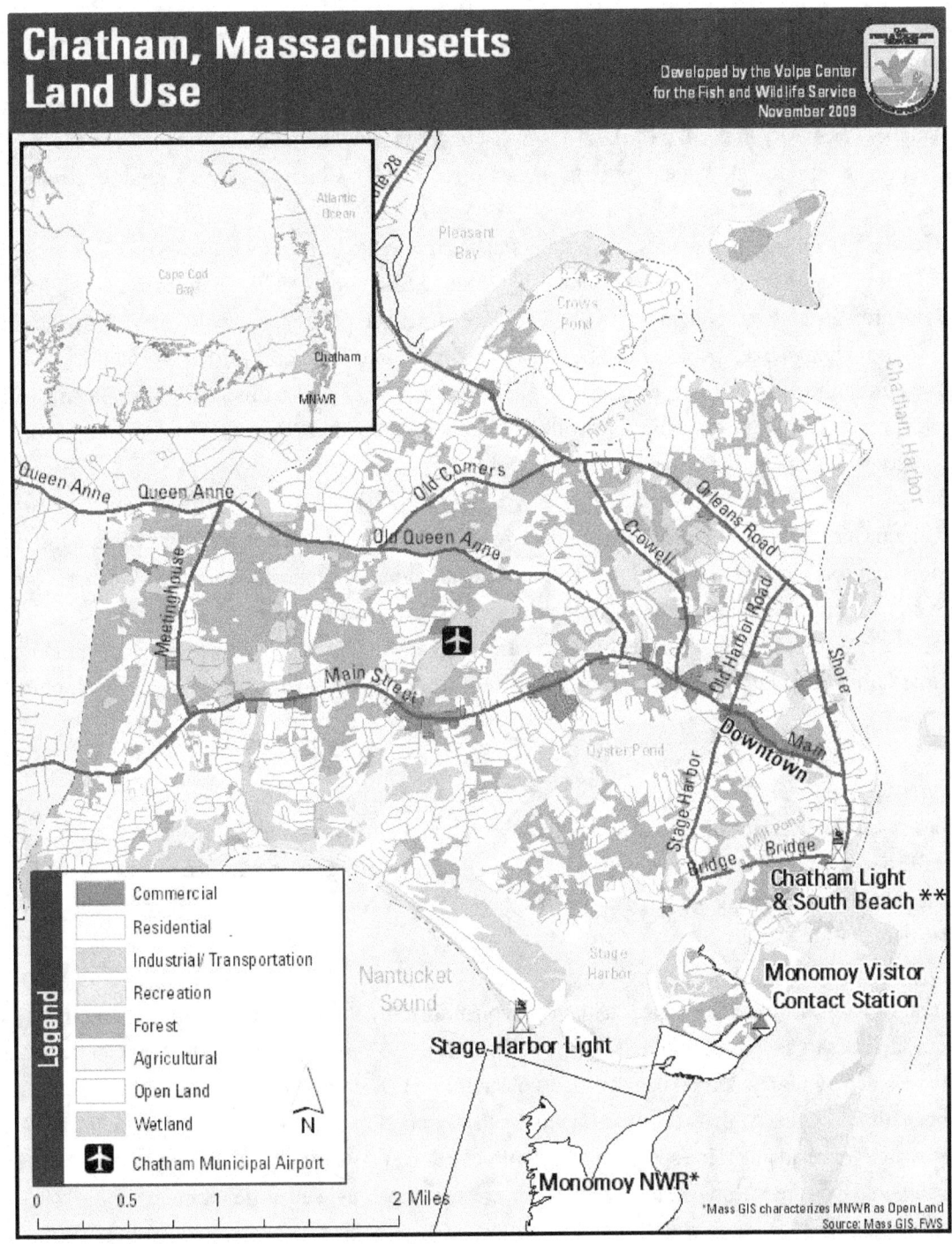

** on this and all subsequent maps, this refers to the Chatham Lighthouse, the town-maintained Lighthouse Beach, and the portion of South Beach connecting to South Monomoy Island.

The recent increase of residential and commercial development has led to a loss of open space, from more than 60 percent of the land in 1960 to less than 30 percent today. Since a building boom in the 1980s, the town has focused on preservation of open space. The town has purchased numerous packages of underdeveloped lands for conservation and watershed. Today, over 1,000 acres on the mainland (approximately 12 percent of the total mainland acreage) are owned publicly or privately as conservation lands.[8] In addition, another 1,000 acres remain undeveloped, primarily in small parcels. A primary concern is how to maintain and preserve the current character and natural environment, while providing an economic base for Chatham's year-round residents.

In 2000, the Cape Cod Commission, working in partnership with the Massachusetts Executive Office of Environmental Affairs, conducted a "build-out" analysis for all 15 Cape towns. This analysis examined local zoning and other growth-related regulations currently in place and made projections about future growth based on the amount of remaining developable land. The analysis revealed that, with no additional growth management or land-protection efforts, the Cape could add 37,000 houses and at least 50,000 people at build-out. Moreover, at current growth rates, build-out will likely be reached within 30 years— within the time horizon of most long range planning efforts.[9]

The 2003 Chatham Comprehensive Plan expresses the strong desire of Chatham residents to maintain the character of neighborhood centers and guard against increased dominance of the automobile. This means, in part, focusing on pedestrian and bicycle safety and limiting both strip development and parking lot construction. Decisions related to development in Chatham are reviewed by the seven-person elected Planning Board. The Board primarily addresses and makes decisions on issues related to zoning and new development requests.

Air and Water Issues

Cape Cod is a non-attainment area for ozone and air quality is continuously monitored by the Massachusetts Department of Environmental Protection at the Truro air quality monitoring station. In general, efforts to limit or reduce personal vehicle usage are a high priority from both a traffic congestion management as well as air quality perspective.

Development on the Cape in general, and in Chatham, is constrained by the ability of the public drinking water and wastewater facilities to adequately serve the population. While the existing housing stock in Chatham can accommodate between 16,000 to 35,000 people, their consumption can strain the local water infrastructure. The aquifer beneath the peninsula that feeds the Cape's freshwater ponds and streams provides the only potable water source for residents. This supply is at risk of pollution and possible depletion in localized areas. Kettle ponds and wetlands are threatened by demands for greater access, as well as development and manipulation.[10]

---

[8] Chatham, Massachusetts Long Range Comprehensive Plan. Town of Chatham
[9] Cape Cod Region Comprehensive Economic Development Strategy. Cape Cod Commission
[10] Cape Cod National Seashore General Management Plan, National Park Service

The Chatham Water Department receives water from nine groundwater wells located within the boundaries of the town of Chatham.[11] The areas immediately around each well (Zone I) are tightly controlled and limited to water supply activities. The areas that are the primary recharge for the aquifer, Zone II, are primarily forested or residential, with smaller areas of commercial, industrial, and waste disposal land uses. Such uses can pose some threat of contamination. For example, residential threats might result from improperly maintained or failing septic systems, household hazardous waste, leaking storage oil tanks, and stormwater. Transportation threats are typically related to gasoline or oil spills, illegally dumped chemicals, or de-icing salt in stormwater.

The town adopted Water Resource Protection Zoning Bylaws in 1996 for the protection of the water within all its Zone II areas. This bylaw limits the type of new or expanded land uses that are permitted within the Zone II areas. Water quality is tested every year to ensure that contaminant levels do not exceed Federal and State drinking water standards.

Special Conservation Areas
The majority of the land area in Chatham is zoned for single family, residential use. Some of the residential areas are also Seashore Conservation districts, with additional restrictions in order to project the Cape Cod National Seashore.

Conservancy Districts are overlay districts intended to:
- Preserve and maintain the ground water supply on which the inhabitants depend;
- Protect the purity of coastal and inland waters for the propagation of fish and shellfish and for recreational purposes;
- Protect the public health and safety;
- Protect persons and property from the hazards of flood and tidal waters resulting from unsuitable development in or near swamps, ponds, bogs and marshes, along water courses or in areas subject to flooding, extreme high tides and the rising sea level; and
- Preserve the amenities of the town and to conserve natural conditions, wildlife and open space for the education and general welfare of the public.

The Conservancy regulations apply to all submerged areas. While the designated Conservancy districts are not located in the areas immediately near MNWR or Lighthouse Beach, their presence in Chatham highlights the importance of conservation in general.

Chatham also has a state-designated Area of Critical Environmental Concern (ACEC) located around the Pleasant Bay. The area, shown in Map 5, includes wetlands and water bodies that outflow into Pleasant Bay. The area includes over 1,000 acres of salt marsh and hundreds of acres of tidal flats in the four towns surrounding the bay (Brewster, Chatham, Harwich, and Orleans). Other important habitats include islands, salt and freshwater ponds, rivers, bays, and barrier beaches. Because of the fishing and tourism opportunities

---

[11] Source Water Assessment and Protection (SWAP) Report. Town of Chatham

provided in the area, these industries are important to the local economy. The designation of the ACEC led to a special Resource Management Plan focusing on protection and maintaining public access. Development in the area is strictly limited.

Map 5: Chatham Area of Critical Environmental Concern

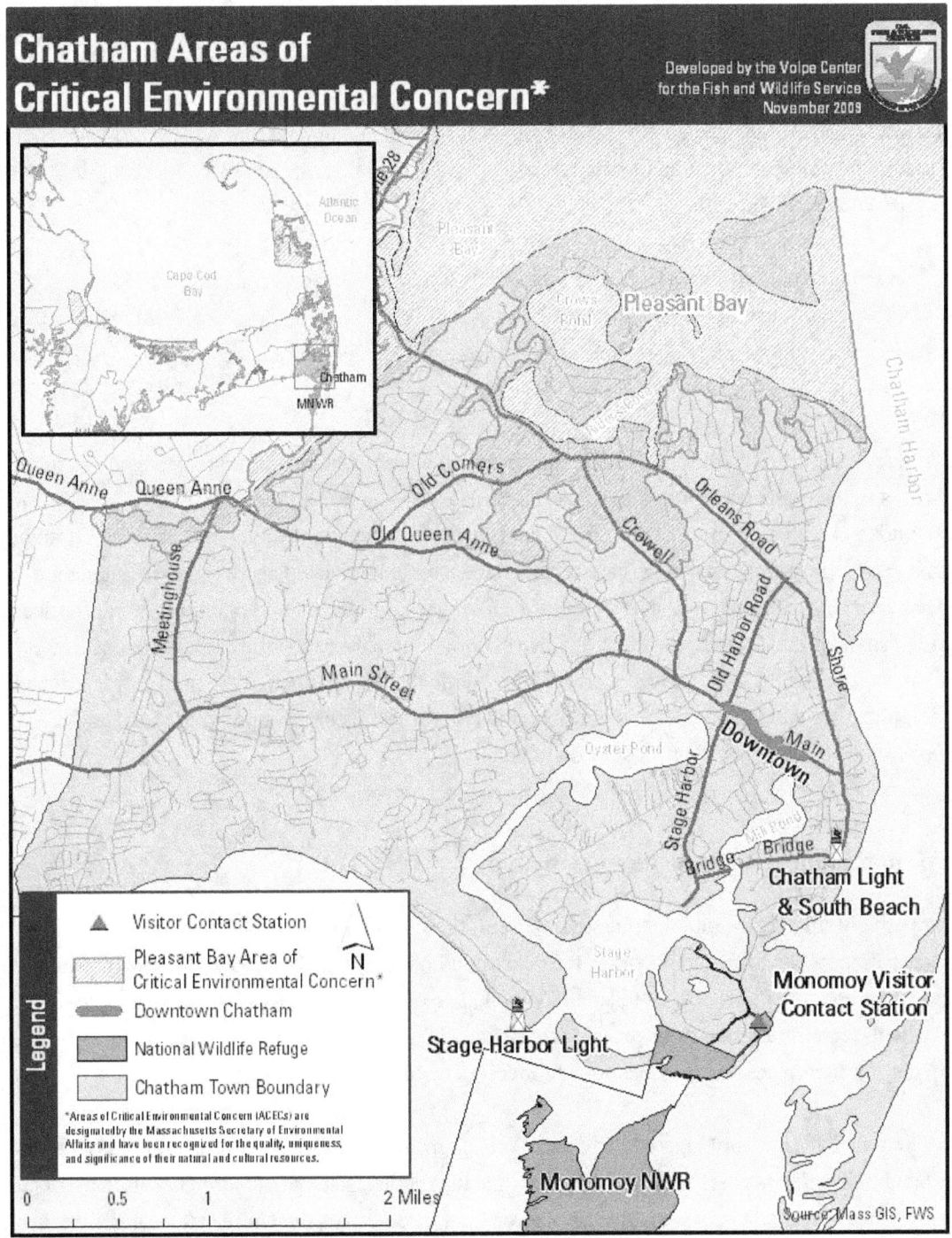

Land Development

Most of the land in Chatham is already built out or identified for conservation, leaving relatively little land available for development. The scarcity of available open land is one contributing factor to the relatively high land cost in Chatham. Given the land availability constraints as well as the desire to limit automobile dominance, there is little appetite in Chatham for building or paving new parking areas. Similarly, development patterns that feature small setbacks, as well as the general sentiment that wider roadways could diminish the community character that gives Chatham much of its appeal, make roadway widening in Chatham unattractive and unlikely.

This existing development patterns influences and is influenced by the transportation network. The predominance of relatively narrow two-lane roads, limited sidewalks, and limited on-street parking establishes some boundaries for this study in identifying and exploring various transportation alternatives.

MNWR and Neighborhood

The area immediately surrounding the MNWR Headquarters on Morris Island comprises privately-owned residences. Access to the site is via a right of way over a private road owned by the neighborhood association. This arrangement is not typical of most FWS refuges, and can be a source of tension between MNWR and the surrounding neighbors. Two important issues are residential encroachments and access road maintenance. There have been concerns from MNWR staff in recent years regarding fencing and plantings along the access road to MNWR, which effectively narrow the roadway (making it narrower than the easement), and could make it more difficult for wider vehicles to access the site. While the road is open to the public, it is privately owned. The neighbors are concerned about the number and type of vehicles traveling on the road and the associated implications for frequency and cost of maintenance.

Demographic and Economic Characteristics

Chatham is a relatively small community, home to 6,625 full time residents.[12] During the summer, the town experiences population swells to five to six times the year-round population.[13] Although the year-round, retirement and summer populations coexist reasonably well, there appears to be a disparity in income between the groups. While the full time residents have a median household income of $45,519 or are retirees, the summer residents are often from communities with higher median incomes.[14]

Table 2 shows that median household income in Chatham is slightly lower than the average in Massachusetts; however, median home value is nearly $100,000 higher than the median for Massachusetts. This suggests that those purchasing homes in Chatham have a greater income than those across the entire state. Therefore, it can be assumed that full-time Chatham residents are not the only individuals purchasing homes in Chatham and that many home purchasers have considerably higher than median income.

---

[12] 2000 US Census
[13] MNWR TAG Report, Inter-Agency TAG Session
[14] 2000 Decennial Census, Summary File 3, population tables, US Census

Table 2: Chatham, Barnstable County, and Massachusetts Income and Housing[15]

	Chatham	Barnstable County	Massachusetts
Median Household Income	$45,519	$45,933	$50.502
Median Home Value	$273,900	$178,800	$185,700
Owner Occupied Housing	80.0%	77.8%	61.7%
Renter Occupied Housing	20.0%	22.2%	33.8%

As shown in Table 3, 34.3 percent of Chatham residents are aged 65 and over, which is relatively high compared with the statewide percentage of 13.5 percent. The large number retirement age residents combined with the average household size of only 2.00, compared with an average 2.51 statewide (as shown in Table 4) suggest that Chatham is a popular retirement community.

Table 3: Chatham, Barnstable County, and Massachusetts Age Distribution[16]

	Chatham	Barnstable County	Massachusetts
Median Age	53.9	44.6	36.5
Under 5 Years Old	2.9%	4.8%	6.3%
18 Years and over	86.7%	79.6%	76.4%
65 Years and over	34.3%	23.1%	13.5%

Table 4: Chatham, Barnstable County, and Massachusetts Population and Household Size[17]

	Chatham	Barnstable County	Massachusetts
Total Population	6,625	222,230	6,349,097
Household Size	2.00	2.28	2.51

Employment and Access

The 2000 U.S. Census estimated 3,645 workers in Chatham. Nearly all of these workers live in Chatham or in other communities on Cape Cod[18].

---

[15] Ibid.
[16] Ibid.
[17] Ibid.
[18] MCD/County-To-MCD/County Worker Flow Files , U.S. Census Bureau

Table 5 shows the distribution of home residence for Chatham workers.

Table 5: Home Communities of Chatham Workers

Home Community	Number of Workers	Percent of Total
Chatham	1,715	47%
Other Cape Cod	1,800	49%
Other	130	4%
Total	**3,645**	**100%**

Similarly, a large percentage of Chatham residents who are employed, work in Chatham or other communities on the Cape. Approximately 61 percent of the 2,815 working Chatham residents are employed in Chatham; another 31 percent are employed in other communities on Cape Cod.

The employment figures indicate that there are roughly 3,000 employees commuting into or out of Chatham on a regular basis. The ability of these people to access their places of work is important, as is the availability of the transportation system to accommodate other personal and recreational travel. One of the goals of this study is to explore various transportation issues, even those that are not currently considered to be problematic, and develop approaches to prevent problems accessing the refuge and beaches before they reach a "crisis." The tourism industry is very important both in Chatham and elsewhere on Cape Cod and this study recognizes the importance of maintaining the general health of the recreation and tourism industries, and promoting access to such attractions.

Tourism

Like many other communities on Cape Cod, the local economy in Chatham depends heavily on tourism, which further highlights the importance of preserving the local character and natural environment. Approximately 38 percent of the 257 business establishments in Chatham are related to the tourism industry (food & drink, lodging, and retail). In 2006, Chatham had 15 lodging establishments, 25 eating/drinking establishments, and 58 retailers.[19] While many of these establishments surely serve the year-round population, they also depend on business from visitors.

In 2007, room taxes on overnight accommodations generated over $12.7 million in revenue on Cape Cod, approximately $1.3 million of which was in Chatham. Table 6 shows the total revenue for all of the Barnstable County communities; the share to Chatham comprises approximately 11 percent of the value for the Cape.

---

[19] Zip Code Business Patterns. U.S. Census Bureau

Table 6: Revenue from Barnstable County 5.7 percent Room Tax[20]

Town/County	FY2007	FY07 % of total
Barnstable	$2,298,759	19.1%
Bourne	$119,234	1.0%
Brewster	$775,266	6.4%
Chatham	$1,341,270	11.2%
Dennis	$564,171	4.7%
Eastham	$377,173	3.1%
Falmouth	$1,333,937	11.1%
Harwich	$562,482	4.7%
Mashpee	$104,696	0.9%
Orleans	$285,631	2.4%
Provincetown	$1,350,204	11.2%
Sandwich	$306,142	2.5%
Truro	$430,297	3.6%
Wellfleet	$159,258	1.3%
Yarmouth	$2,016,600	16.8%
Barnstable County	$12,025,120	100.0%
Massachusetts	$157,515,000	

Economic Benefits of Monomoy to Local Communities

In 2006, FWS conducted a study to measure the economic benefit of refuge visitation on local communities. The study, "Banking on Nature," provided descriptions and in-depth data on 80 refuges around the country, including MNWR. The study used data from the Fish and Wildlife Service National Survey of Fishing, Hunting, and Wildlife-Associated Recreation (NSFHWR) and the FWS Refuge Annual Performance Plan (RAPP) to develop a profile of refuge visitors' spending in local communities. The analysis estimated visitor expenditures on food, lodging, transportation, and other fees (guide fees, equipment rental, etc.).

---

[20] "Cape Collects $12 Million in State Room Tax." Cape Cod Commission

Table 7 shows the distribution of the estimated 31,660 recreational visits to MNWR in 2006. Non-residents[21] account for nearly 90 percent of total visits.

---

[21] "Residents" are assumed to be residents of the state. This means that for example, visitors from the Boston area, two hours away from the refuge, are also counted as residents.

Table 7: Monomoy NWR 2006 Recreation Visits[22]

Activity	Residents	Non-residents	Total
Non-Consumptive			
Nature Trails	172	1,544	1,716
Observation Platforms	0	0	0
Wildlife Observation	318	2,866	3,184
Beach/Water Use	850	7,650	8,500
Other Recreation*	1,700	15,300	17,000
Fishing			
Freshwater	3	27	30
Saltwater	185	1,046	1,230
Total Visitation	**3,228**	**28,433**	**31,660**

* includes trips to the visitor contact station.

The study estimated that MNWR visitors spent approximately $489,000 on recreational expenditures in Barnstable County in 2006, with non-residents accounting for nearly 97 percent of this spending. Expenditures on non-consumptive activities comprised 91 percent of the spending, compared to 9 percent related to fishing. This leads to jobs, personal income, and municipal tax revenue – an estimated additional $279,800 in economic value for the county.

It is important to note that it is difficult to measure the benefit that the greater Chatham community receives as a result of MNWR. Because MNWR charges no admission and has many access points, some of which are informal, there is no accurate method to measure the number of visitors to the refuge. In addition, there are several private boat tours that travel past the islands to view the seals but do not stop at MNWR. It is not possible to measure the benefit provided by this type of recreation, as the number of tour boat passengers is not publically available.

2.4. Transportation and Traffic

In order to access MNWR, visitors must use a right of way across private land. Visitors may arrive by ferry, automobile, bicycle, or on foot.

The discussion of transportation and traffic issues pertinent to Chatham and MNWR is the basis for this study of alternative access opportunities for reaching the refuge. This study identifies current problems and

---

[22] Banking on Nature. FWS.

approaches to address those problems, as well as approaches to managing transportation issues before they reach a crisis stage or are more difficult to address in the future.

Some of the information presented is historical, while other data represent a snapshot of conditions during a particular data collection effort or point in time. While existing conditions provide a basis for identifying important patterns and trends, it is important to note that random or infrequent events (such as event storm-related congestion, for example) may result in "outlier" data that are not representative of typical conditions.

Cycling and Pedestrian Activity

Cape Cod bicyclists and pedestrians are served by a network of paved trails, state-designated bicycle routes, and sidewalks.

Sidewalks

More than 90 percent of Cape Cod roads do not have sidewalks.[23] Many of the roads without sidewalks are located in residential and/or non-urban neighborhoods where traffic is light. Given the narrow roadway widths and buildings often set close to the road, the majority of roadways in Chatham do not have sidewalks. There are sidewalks on at least one side of the street on Main Street and around the Lighthouse and Lighthouse Beach, but they do not extend to Bridge Street. There are no sidewalks on the roughly one mile stretch between the MNWR Headquarters and the Chatham Lighthouse.

Cape Cod Rail Trail

The Cape Cod Rail Trail (CCRT) is a converted rail grade that runs from Dennis to Wellfleet, passing through Harwich, Brewster, Orleans, and Eastham. It includes an extension from Harwich to Chatham. The main line of the trail is 21.9 miles, and the Chatham branch is 6.2 miles. The terminus of the Chatham branch is located approximately 3.5 miles from MNWR. The Massachusetts Department of Conservation and Recreation (DCR), which owns and maintains the trail, estimates that 400,000 people use the trail annually. The full Cape Cod Rail Trail system is shown below in Map 6.

---

[23] Cape Cod 2007 Regional Transportation Plan. Cape Cod Commission

Map 6: Existing Bicycle Network on Lower/Outer Cape Cod

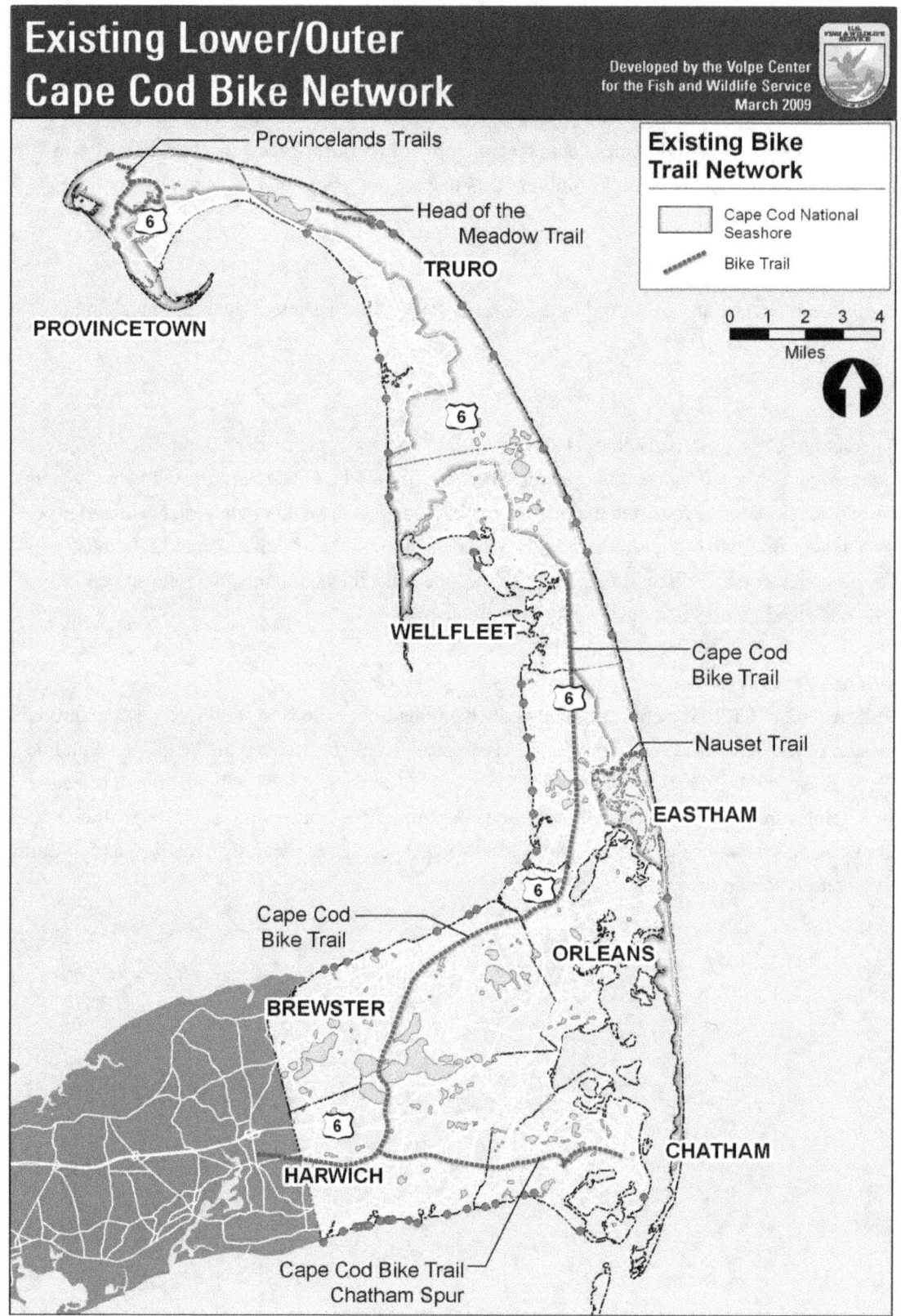

Bicycle Routes

A bicycle route is any road, path, or trail that has been designated for bicycle use. In many cases, these are side streets with a low volume of traffic or roads with wide shoulders. Roadways designated for bicycle usage are able to link paths where bicycle rights-of-way are limited or unavailable. There are several signed bicycle routes in Chatham, connecting to multiple destinations within Chatham and to neighboring towns. These routes avoid the heavily congested downtown portion of Main Street but do access Lighthouse Beach. The Chatham Bikeways Committee has developed maps showing the off-road paths in Chatham and the signed bicycle routes. These are shown below in Figure 1 and Figure 2.

Figure 1: Bike Trails and Routes in Chatham

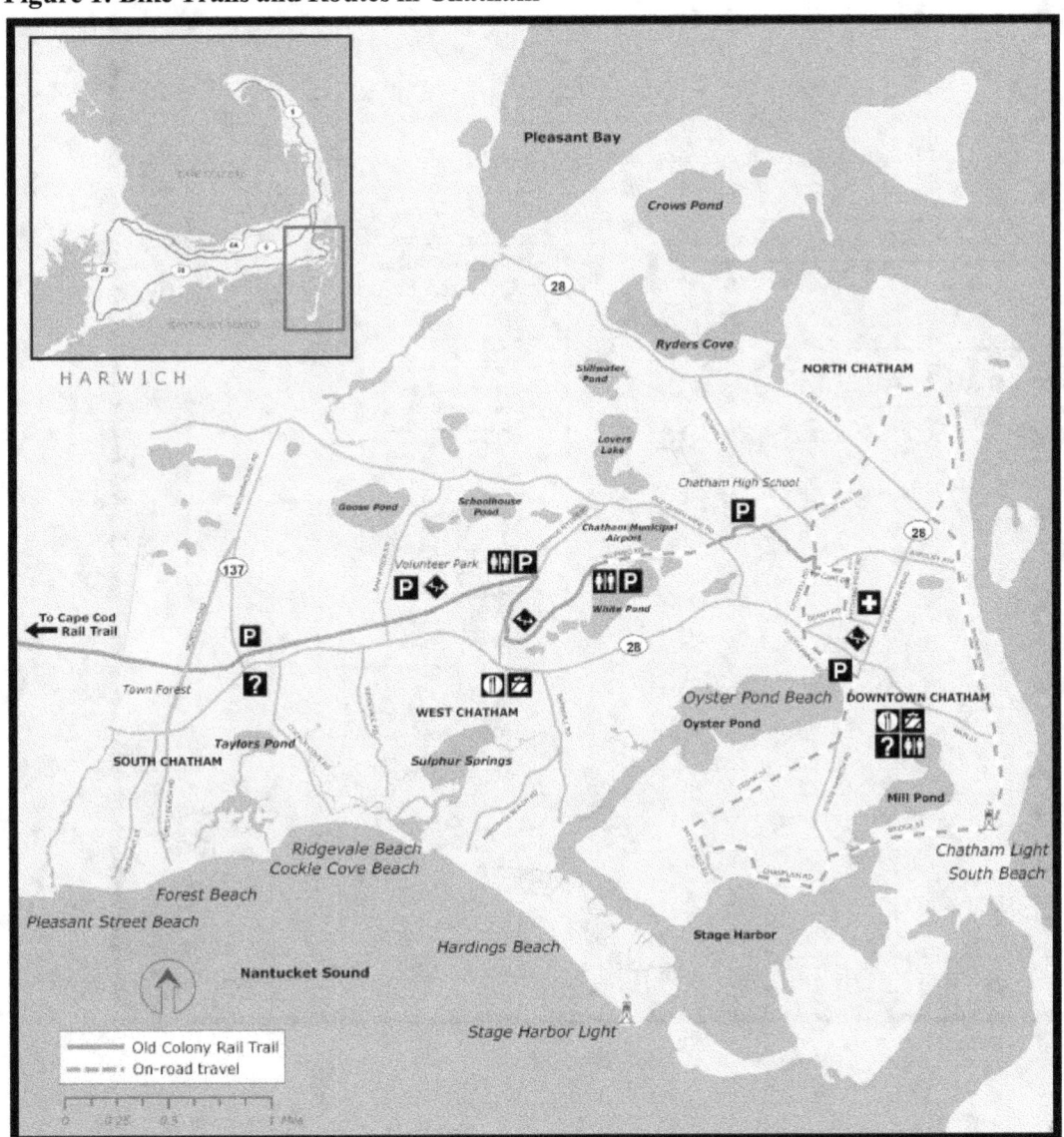

Source: Chatham Bikeways Commission

Figure 2: Downtown Chatham Bicycle Trails and Routes

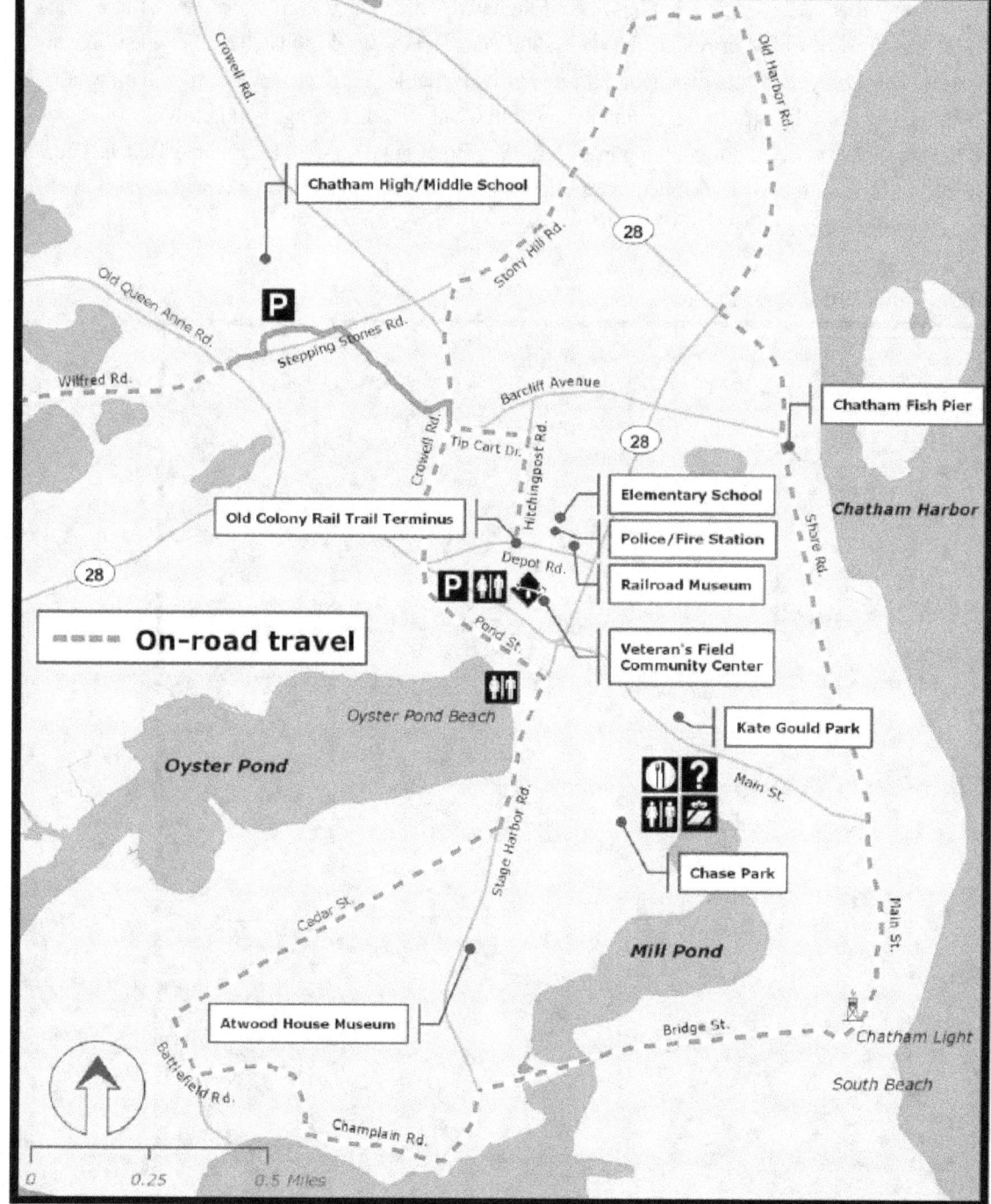

Source: Chatham Bikeways Commission

Signage and Wayfinding

The absence of both directional and informational signage can make MNWR difficult to locate. There are no signs off the highway or in Chatham directing visitors or informing potential visitors about MNWR until just before the entrance. A further complication is that the Morris Island parcel with the headquarters/visitor contact station is located beyond a gate that identifies the private roads of the Quitnesset neighborhood. The lack of adequate signage has several negative impacts: it can deter and discourage visitors and can cause confused visitors to accidentally drive through private neighborhoods while trying to find the headquarters/visitor contact station.

Additionally, one of the ferry landings that provides access to the islands is situated at the end of a road marked as a "Dead End." The access to the other ferry, located at the headquarters/visitor contact station, has a sign for the ferry service but not for the headquarters/visitor contact station.

Signs to Monomoy ferries

Vehicular Traffic and Circulation

Automobile traffic and congestion in Chatham has increased with the region's population. Between 1990 and 2000, the population of Barnstable County grew by approximately 20 percent, to a total of 222,230 residents.[24] According to the Cape Cod Commission, average daily crossings of the Sagamore and Bourne Bridges now exceed the peak summer crossings of two decades ago.

---

[24]Cape Cod Commission Data. U.S. Census Bureau

Table 8 shows average year-round and summer crossings for selected years since 1985.

Table 8: Average Daily Bridge Crossings, 1985-2008[25]

Year	Average Daily Crossings (year-round)	Average Daily Crossings (summer peak)
1985	63,014	90,241
1990	81,388	114,250
1995	86,879	119,888
2000	95,637	125,889
2005	96,155	128,137
2008	93,415	123,346

This resulting congestion is a concern to Chatham, given its popularity as a destination and its narrow roadways. Roadway widening – a common approach to address automobile congestion – is not usually considered in Chatham. This is mainly due to development patterns that feature small setbacks, as well as the general sentiment that wider roadways could diminish the community character that gives Chatham much of its appeal.

Traffic congestion in Chatham in general, and specifically around the MNWR area, is primarily seasonal. Traffic during the summer months is estimated to be 25 to 30 percent higher than the average during the year.[26] Summer traffic congestion has a significant impact on the downtown Main Street area for two primary reasons. First, Main Street features many small shops, attractions, and other destinations. Second, most visitors attempting to access Lighthouse Beach and MNWR must pass through the downtown area.

The 2007 Cape Cod Regional Transportation Plan indicates that even though Chatham and its neighboring communities are generally less congested than other parts of Barnstable County, "certain road segments such as Main Street in Chatham, west of downtown, operate well over capacity during peak hours." The town of Chatham is also wary of growing congestion. Its 2003 comprehensive plan states that "Chathamites...firmly want to protect against...increased dominance of the automobile encouraging strip development, requiring more parking lots [sic], undermining the character of neighborhood centers, and threatening the safety of pedestrians and bicyclists."

Morris Island

Traffic counts around Morris Island Road have found an average of approximately 1,300 cars per day during the peak summer season. This includes traffic to the Monomoy Headquarters, the adjacent neighborhoods, the causeway, and the dock. The peak hour traffic volume is approximately 150 cars.

At the intersection of Morris Island Road and Wikis Way, at the entrance to the Monomoy headquarters/visitor contact station, turning movement traffic counts in August 2008 observed 88 cars during the peak hour (around

---

[25] Cape Cod Traffic Counting Report. Cape Cod Commission
[26] Cape Cod Traffic Counting: Chatham Traffic Counts: 1998-2008. Cape Cod Commission

10:30am on Friday). Of the 88 cars, slightly fewer than half (43) were turning to and from the refuge, while slightly more than half (45) were going straight to and from the Quitnesset neighborhood. During the same hour, 11 people were observed walking and 13 bicycling through the intersection, though their destinations are not known.

Traffic counts are predictably low given Morris Island's location. More noteworthy is the fact that almost half of all automobiles traversing the intersection of Morris Island Road and the Monomoy headquarters entrance were going to or coming from the headquarters/visitor contact station, indicating that although total traffic volume is low, Monomoy accounts for about half of it.

Lighthouse and Bridge Street Area
Traffic counts on Bridge Street have found upwards of 3,000 cars per day and up to 300 cars during peak hours. These cars may be accessing a variety of destinations – neighborhoods off Bridge Street, traffic passing through to boating areas and the town beach, and those parking to visit Lighthouse Beach.

Closer to the Lighthouse, observed traffic counts are somewhat higher. Counts have found over 4,000 vehicles per day during the summer, and over 600 vehicles at the intersection of Main Street and Shore Road during the peak hour in August 2008. Of the vehicles in the intersection, approximately 60 percent (419) were traveling to or from the area around the Lighthouse, while approximately 40 percent (270) were traveling between the downtown area and Shore Road. During this same hour, over 100 pedestrians and 50 bicyclists were also observed at this intersection. Congestion at this intersection is a particular problem for cyclists and pedestrians given narrow road width and lack of sidewalks. Reducing congestion at this intersection would be particularly beneficial to these roadway users.

Main Street
Downtown Main Street accommodates high levels of through-traffic as well as serving as a primary destination. Residents and visitors seek access to the shops, restaurants, and lodging that form Chatham's economic base, as well as to other points in town served by this important corridor. Annually, more than 10,000 cars travel on Main Street every day; the counts typically exceed 13,000 in the summer months. In the summer, nearly 1,000 cars have been observed in the peak hour. Main Street frequently operates at or near capacity, and may experience further pressure from cars looking for parking and from heavy pedestrian activity. Because of Main Street's dual status as destination and travel corridor, strategies for alleviating congestion will likely also improve access to Lighthouse Beach and Monomoy.

Main Street, Chatham

Traffic Safety

The Chatham Police Department (CPD) maintains data related to traffic accidents and violations throughout the town, including at the following locations near Monomoy and Lighthouse Beach:

- Shore Road and Main Street, Chatham, MA
- Morris Island Road and Bridge Street, Chatham, MA

The data include raw numbers of traffic accidents, speeding violations, protective custody incidents, and parking complaints. For the five year period between October 21, 2003 and October 21, 2008, the most common violations have been for speeding at the intersection of Main Street and Shore Road during the five year period (29 violations). Annual recorded violations varied, peaking at eleven in the first year and dropping to two violations in the last year. During that same period there were two traffic accidents, one speeding violation, and three parking complaints reported for the intersection of Morris Island Road and Bridge Street.

These data do not include stops by police that resulted in warnings, but rather, issued tickets and violations or reported incidents and accidents. According to the CPD, many verbal warnings are issued for traffic violations. During peak tourist season, there tend to be fewer speeding violations because increased traffic congestion and pedestrian activity do not allow for high traffic speeds. Parking complaints do not always lead to tickets, but sometimes result in multiple tickets. The CPD cites seasonal visitors as a major source of violations at the surveyed intersections, given the proximity to public beaches and tourist attractions.

The traffic safety data measure only annual levels; they do not highlight peak periods. While there are relatively few annual violations, parking and traffic congestion consistently concern residents and other local stakeholders. One explanation may be that the parking and congestion problems that neighbors find to be a nuisance do not actually result in violations.

Parking

Monomoy Headquarters

The Monomoy headquarters/visitor contact station parking area currently holds 35-40 cars.[27] It was expanded from 11 spaces to 35 in 2001 and tends to fill to capacity during the peak season. Space constraints limit the ability to further expand the parking lot. Although there is no official data, the lot seems to turn over fairly quickly with most visitors departing within one to two hours.

The lot includes two spaces for oversized vehicles. Approximately ten tour buses visit each year and must obtain a special permit from the refuge. School buses usually notify the refuge in advance of their arrival, but do not need special permits. Recreational vehicles are typically instructed to park on the causeway.

Rip Ryder, one of the two ferry operators licensed by the refuge, uses the parking lot at the headquarters/visitor contact station[28] and passengers walk down a staircase to the water to access the boat. If the parking lot is full, passengers can park on the causeway and either ride the shuttle van or walk back to the headquarters/visitor contact station. Rip Ryder carries approximately 50 passengers per month during peak season.

In an effort to better understand Monomoy visitor origins, the study team conducted a pilot effort to collect visitor information over the Columbus Day holiday weekend in 2008. Between 11:20 AM and 11:30 AM on Sunday the Cape Cod Commission recorded the state origins of the license plates on automobiles parked in the Monomoy Headquarters parking lot. The license plate numbers for Massachusetts vehicles were compared with data from a Registry of Motor Vehicle database in order to identify the town in which each vehicle was registered. This database was most recently updated in February 2008.

While data from one point in time during the "shoulder season" cannot be used to draw significant conclusions, they do offer some insight regarding visitation to the refuge. There were 24 cars in the parking lot, though the visitor contact station was not open. The breakdown of vehicle state origin is shown below in

---

[27] MNWR TAG Report, Inter-Agency TAG Session
[28] The Outermost ferry, which also brings passengers to the islands, leaves from and has parking at a different site. More discussion of ferry service is found in Section 1.3.6.

Table 9:

Table 9: Snapshot of MNWR Headquarters/Visitor Contact Station Parking

State	Number	Percent
RI	2	8.3
CT	3	12.5
NY	3	12.5
ME	2	8.3
MA	14	58.3
Total	**24**	**100.0**

Of the 12 Massachusetts vehicles whose information was found in the database, only one was registered in Chatham and only two were registered elsewhere in Barnstable County. Eight were registered in the Greater Boston area. There were 10 vehicles registered outside of Massachusetts, with origins in other northeast states of Rhode Island, Connecticut, Maine, and New York. It should be noted that it is possible that vehicles with out of state plates could belong to people with vacation homes in Chatham or other Cape Cod communities.

While this data collection effort was limited, it showed that such information is relatively easy to obtain, and there is value in establishing a baseline level of data that could be regularly updated. Regular information about numbers and origins of vehicles in the headquarters/visitor contact station lot may assist in developing approaches for alternative access to the lot, and in identifying the best strategies for disseminating information about alternative access.

Morris Island Road Causeway

The town-owned Morris Island Road causeway (referred to as the Causeway) adjacent to Morris Island holds approximately 80-85 cars and can reach up to 85 percent capacity during the summer months.[29] The Causeway has no shoulder, requiring vehicles to park partially in the travel lane, effectively reducing the roadway to 1.5 lanes. According to FWS staff, emergency responders have reported problems responding to residential and refuge needs when Causeway parking is filled.

---

[29] MNWR TAG Report, Inter-Agency TAG Session

Causeway, with parking and a passing car

Those who park on the Causeway are not necessarily all visitors to the refuge. Chatham's parking surveys have found that approximately one-third of users are shellfishermen, one-third are kayakers, and the remaining third are refuge visitors. The Causeway is located on a dredge spoil and could physically be widened, though residents have opposed past plans to construct more formal parking areas along it.

Lighthouse Beach

There is limited parking available for visitors to Lighthouse Beach. There are 48 spaces right at the beach and the lighthouse, with a 30-minute time limit. Because of congestion levels and the time limit, many beach visitors elect to park on Bridge Street and walk to the beach. The area on Bridge Street that is open to parking can hold approximately 80 cars and is frequently over 85 percent capacity during the summer months.[30] The parking area is located roughly one-half mile from the beach and most of the road is narrow, windy, and without sidewalks. Given the parking constraints, it is not uncommon for visitors parked at the Lighthouse Beach lot to intentionally overstay the 30-minute limit and elect to pay the fine, according to Chatham police.

---

[30] MNWR TAG Report, Inter-Agency TAG Session

Walking between Bridge Street and beach

Parking by the lighthouse

Parking on Bridge Street

Parking on Bridge Street

In the fall of 2008, the town selectmen voted to require a window sticker for any car parking on Bridge Street. The sticker fee is $15 per day, though other town stickers available to residents and property owners will also be accepted. Signs posted along Bridge Street will indicate the hours during which the stickers are required, the $50 violation fine and direct visitors to sticker purchase locations. Because the sticker requirement did not take effect until July 2009, the long term impacts on parking around Lighthouse Beach are still unclear.

Another relatively new development related to Lighthouse Beach is that in January 2009, the Chatham Board of Health voted to prohibit swimming at the beach, due to fast currents and several incidents of drowning in recent years. This decision was later revised to allow "swim at your own risk" access to the beach, with no lifeguards provided, and beach patrols available to assess conditions, educate the public, and prevent and respond to emergencies.

The effects of the parking sticker and lifeguard decisions are not yet known; these two actions highlight the fact that external decisions may impact visitation and access to Monomoy.

Municipally-Owned Parking

In downtown Chatham, there are four municipally-owned parking lots with a total of 254 parking spaces. On-street parking on Main Street provides approximately 130 spaces.[31] The breakdown of parking spaces is shown below in Table 10. In the peak summer season, the majority of these spaces are typically occupied.

Table 10: Municipally Owned Parking

Facility	Spaces	Distance From MNWR HQ (miles)
Main St (on-street)	130	~2.5
Town Hall	88	2.3
Stage Harbor Lot (behind Colonial Bldg / CVS)	105	2.5
Off Main St (behind Chatham Squire)	35	2.2
Kate Gould Park	26	2.2

The quarter-mile stretch of Main Street around which the Stage Harbor, Chatham Town Hall, Off Main Street, and Gould Park lots are located is roughly 2.5 miles from the MNWR headquarters/visitor contact station. The four municipally-owned parking facilities are utilized to capacity every day of the week in peak season, which is July and August. In the shoulder seasons (May-June and September-October), there is competition for spaces on weekends but less so on weekdays. Based on information provided by the town, there is little to no available capacity in the downtown parking facilities that could be used as satellite parking during peak season.

---

[31] All municipally owned parking data provided by Chatham Planning Department, 2008.

There is no charge for or use restriction on municipally-owned spaces with one exception: 20 spaces at the Chatham Town Hall are reserved for use by municipal employees between 8:00 AM and 4:00 PM Monday through Friday. Currently, the town is considering a resident sticker program for on-street parking.

There are also several publicly owned parking lots associated with specific facilities. The schools and community center also provide parking; the elementary school and community center are located approximately one-half mile from downtown Main Street (approximately three miles from the headquarters/visitor contact station) and provide a combined 200 parking spaces. The junior and senior high schools, located approximately 1.3 miles from downtown Main Street, have 169 parking spaces on-site. The school parking lots are utilized for school functions during the regular school year, but are generally not utilized to capacity in summer months. School and community parking spaces are shown below in Table 11. The locations of all of the municipally owned public parking facilities are shown in Map 7.

Table 11: School and Community Center Parking

Facility	Spaces	Distance From MNWR HQ (miles)
Community Center	105	2.9
Elementary School	95	2.9
Jr/Sr High School	169	3.7

Map 7: Municipally Owned Parking Facilities

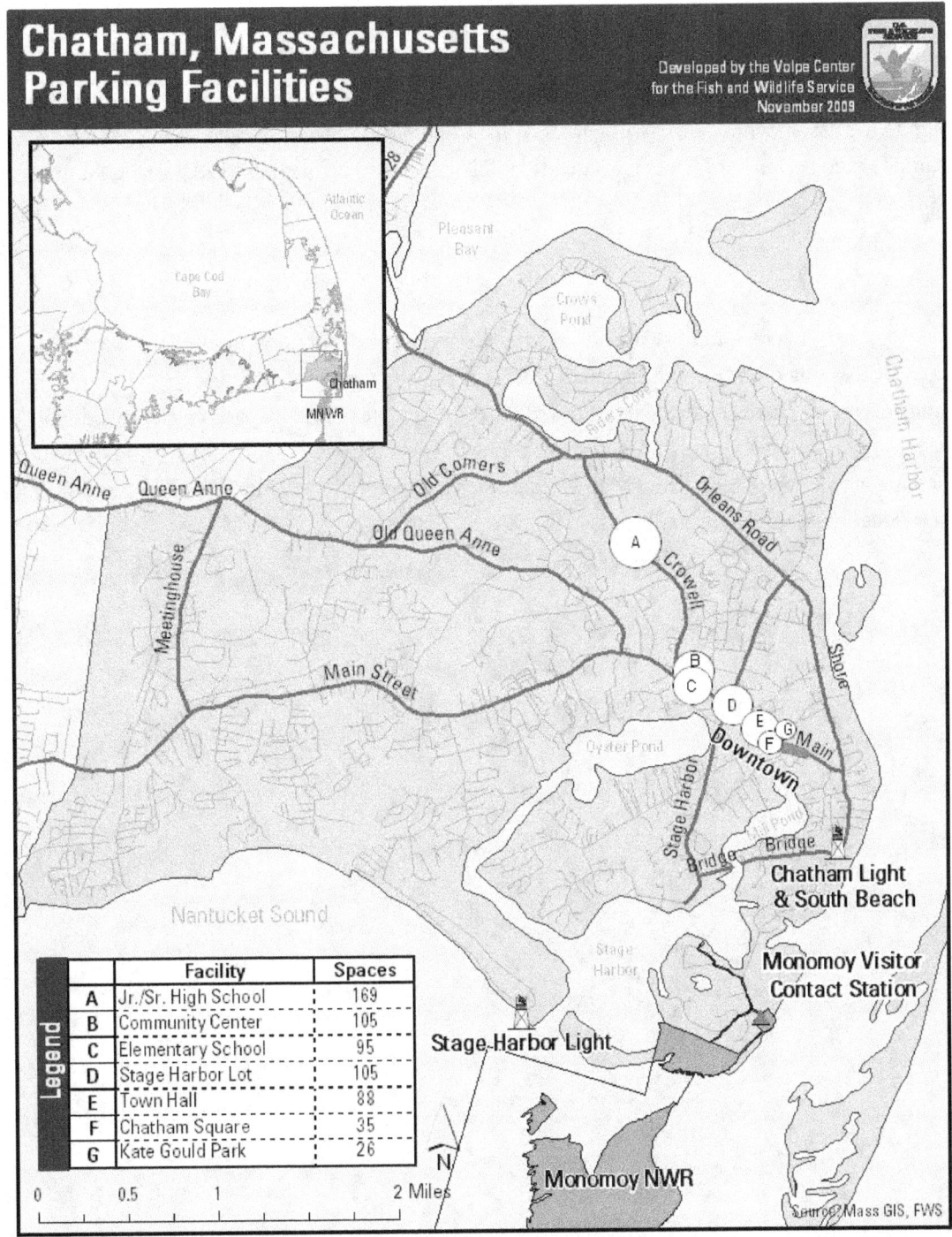

	Facility	Spaces
A	Jr./Sr. High School	169
B	Community Center	105
C	Elementary School	95
D	Stage Harbor Lot	105
E	Town Hall	88
F	Chatham Square	35
G	Kate Gould Park	26

Other Parking

Limited parking options and demand for downtown and beach parking, have led to other creative solutions. For example, owners of a former gas station parking lot on Main Street charge $5 for parking and another $5 to drive small groups of customers to the beach in a station wagon. The lot can hold up to 50 cars and can fill in peak season. Users do not have a time restriction for parking. The proprietors report that some customers park there to go to the beach, while others will park to walk around Main Street, or both. While various schemes for limited paid parking are under consideration, this appears to be the only paid parking lot in Chatham at this time.

Transit

The Cape Cod Regional Transit Authority (CCRTA) operates public transportation throughout Barnstable County with relatively limited service to Chatham. CCRTA service to Chatham includes one fixed route as well as paratransit service. There are also other types of CCRTA services on other parts of Cape Cod that could someday serve as a model for expanded transit options in Chatham. CCRTA routes serving the entire Cape and Chatham are shown in Map 8 and Map 9. These services, as well as private services to and from the Cape, as well as local shuttle services are discussed in the following pages.

Map 8: Cape Cod Regional Transit Authority System

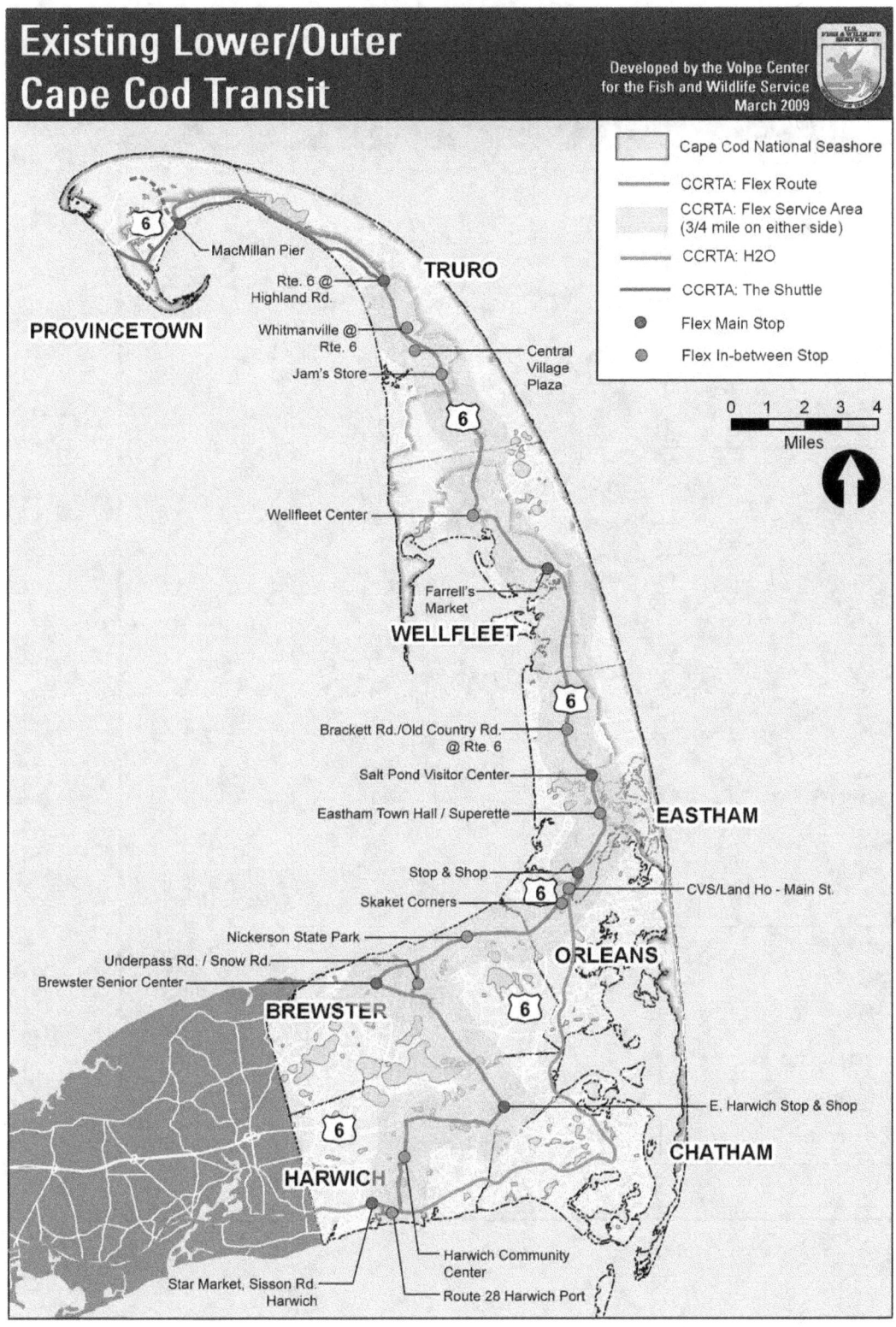

Map 9: CCRTA Service to Chatham

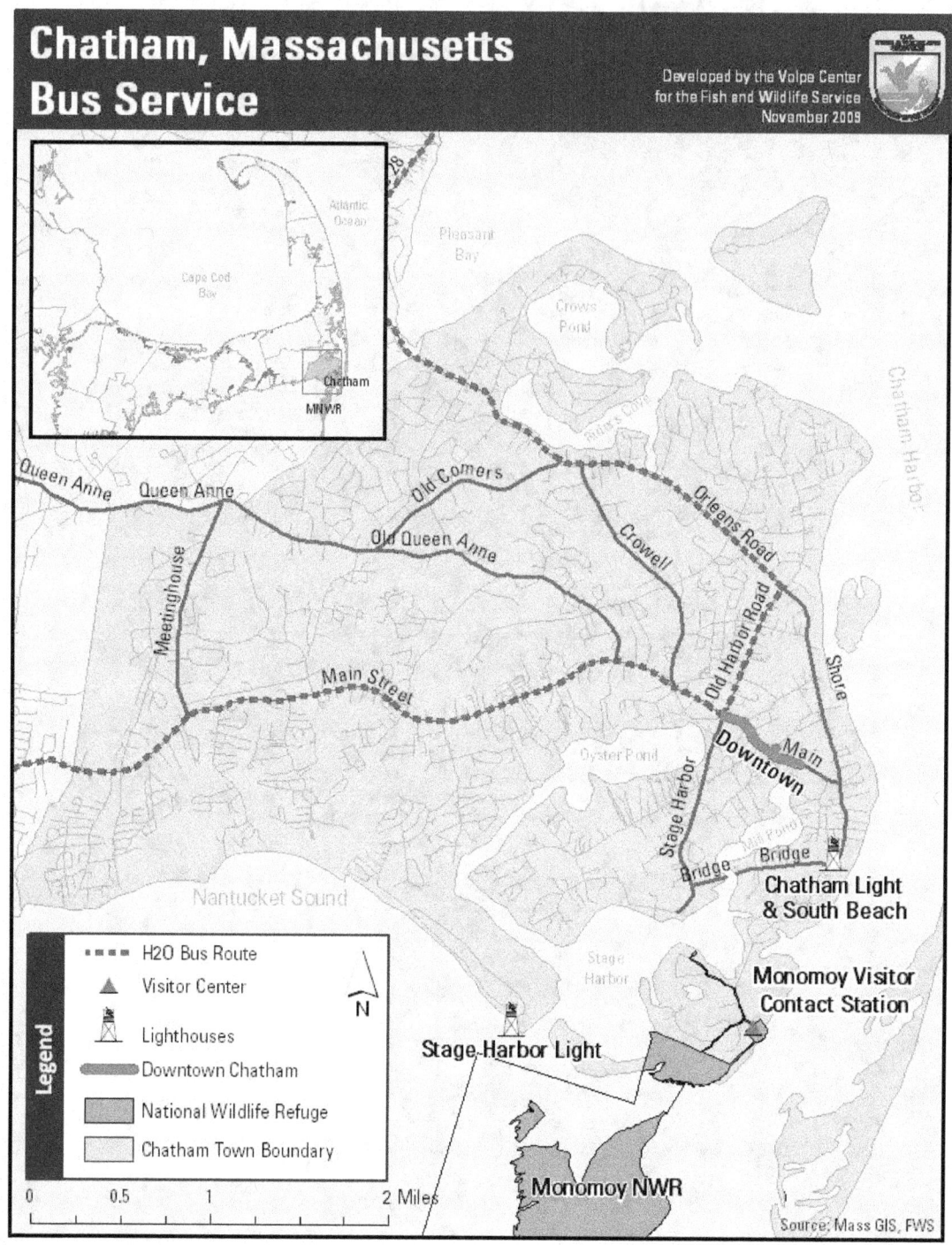

Hyannis to Orleans (H2O)

The H2O route serves the towns of Hyannis, Yarmouth, Dennis, Harwich, Chatham, and Orleans. The schedule currently runs nine buses per day in each direction, with three stops in Chatham. The closest stop to the refuge is approximately 2.25 miles away. In FY08 the line served approximately 84,400 passengers.

B-Bus

The B-Bus is a Cape Cod-wide door-to-door demand-responsive paratransit service. CCRTA provides this ride-by-appointment service for people of all ages for trips of any purpose, including school, work, shopping, college, doctor's appointments, visiting friends, and medical trips to Boston. B-Buses carry up to 19 passengers and are all lift-equipped.

In 2008, demand response service carried 2,586 passengers in Chatham. This represents one percent of the total demand response trips on the Cape. This is an increase of over 1,000 percent from 2007, when only 208 passengers were served.

FlexRoute

FlexRoute is an innovative transit service which operates along a fixed route "centerline" with the ability to pick up and drop off 0.75 miles from the centerline. This allows the FlexRoute to serve more of the population than a typical fixed route and on a more convenient demand response basis.

The FlexRoute began in 2006 and serves the Outer Cape towns of Provincetown, Truro, Wellfleet, Eastham, Orleans, Brewster, and Harwich, as well as the Cape Cod National Seashore. FlexRoute has been very successful to date with ridership numbers higher than initial forecasts. It has served over 60,000 riders each year that it has been operational. FlexRoute does not currently serve Chatham; but converting the H2O line to a Flex-type service has been considered.

Regional and Local Private Bus and Shuttle Services

Transportation to the Cape and, in some cases, within Cape Cod, is also provided by a number of private bus and ferry companies. These companies provide service from throughout New England and New York to Hyannis and Provincetown, from which connections could be made to Chatham.

Chatham Bars Inn's Trolley Bus Shuttle and Antique Car Tour

The Chatham Bars Inn is a luxury resort hotel on Shore Road located approximately two miles north of Monomoy. The Inn offers two recreational transportation services free of charge to its guests – a trolley bus shuttle and an antique car history tour. They are well utilized by Inn guests.

The trolley bus has no fixed route; it takes guests to various destinations in town at their request. Chatham Bars Inn staff estimate that guests request to be taken to the Monomoy headquarters/visitor contact station once or twice a day during peak tourist season. Other popular destinations include the lighthouse, Oyster Pond, and area restaurants. Inn guests typically do not travel to the Monomoy visitor contact station with beach equipment, as the Inn has a private beach on site. Trolley service is offered every day from July through Labor Day and on weekends during the off-season. It has been offered since 2003.

The antique car history tour runs on a fixed route through town, which includes a 10-15 minute stop at Monomoy. It is offered three days a week from mid-June to Labor Day. This service has been offered since 2000.

Ferry, Rail, and Aviation

Refuge Ferry Service

Presently, the only way to access North Monomoy Island and South Monomoy is via private ferry. Some of Chatham's tourist operations will take visitors near the islands to view the wildlife; however, only two companies hold Special Use Permits (SUPs) to operate commercial ferry service landing on the islands. The ferry service is primarily used by tourists, beachgoers, birdwatchers, and fishermen. Each ferry boat holds fewer than 25 passengers.

Rip Ryder van at MNWR headquarters/visitor contact station

Anecdotally, some Chatham residents and visitors believe the ferry service causes traffic congestion issues. The Rip Ryder ferry service currently has an agreement with the refuge for the use of a small number of parking spaces within the headquarters/visitor contact station parking lot for ferry passengers. Overflow passengers can park on the causeway and walk back to the headquarters/visitor contact station or ride the shuttle van to the headquarters/visitor contact station. The ferry departs from the bottom of the stairs at the headquarters/visitor contact station.

The Outermost Adventures ferry service has parking and launches from a site at the end of Seagull Road, on the way to the refuge. Signage and way-finding to the access point can be confusing as the signage indicates that the road is a dead end, but not that the launch site is at the end of the road (see photo in section on signage).

2.5. Conclusions from Existing Conditions Analysis

The following is a recap of the major items identified through the analysis of existing conditions.

- Environmental protection and preservation is a high priority in the town of Chatham.
- The tourism industry is of vital importance to communities on Cape Cod in general, and to Chatham in particular.
- Due primarily to tourism patterns, traffic congestion and other transportation issues in Chatham are highly seasonal.
- Transportation challenges in Chatham could worsen without any intervention – one of the goals of this study is to address challenges before they reach a "crisis" level.
- Existing development patterns and community preservation priorities limit the opportunities for roadway widening, building new parking facilities, and the use of full-size transit vehicles.

Existing conditions data, along with feedback from public involvement efforts, helped the study team determine criteria and identify scenarios for a variety of transportation improvements to MNWR and Lighthouse Beach.

3. STAKEHOLDER INPUT

As part of the research process, the study team solicited opinions, ideas, and suggestions for transportation alternatives from stakeholders in the study area. Stakeholders consist of many different groups, from year-round and seasonal Chatham residents, to the business community, elected officials, town and regional planning staff, and others. The purpose of the outreach efforts is threefold: to provide background information and a project overview, to provide an opportunity for stakeholders to identify high-priority transportation concerns, and to facilitate the identification of potential solutions.

Throughout fiscal years 2010 and 2011, FWS is developing the Comprehensive Conservation Plan (CCP) for MNWR, a process that requires extensive public involvement and review under the National Environmental Protection Act (NEPA). The CCP process addresses a wide variety of issues – including transportation. In this context, the public outreach efforts for the Monomoy Alternative Transportation Study (ATS) were limited to introducing the key transportation issues related to the refuge; the ATS public involvement activities were designed to establish a foundation for more in-depth dialogue during the CCP development.

The Volpe Center study team developed recommendations from the public for involvement strategies. These were reviewed with the study team and carried out during the course of the research project. Outreach efforts included:

- Hosting open meetings with the general public
- Hosting meetings with civic and business leaders
- Facilitating working group sessions with representatives from local and regional governments
- Developing study-specific information and updates posted on the refuge and town of Chatham websites
- Distributing information sheets to Chatham Town Hall and the Chatham Public Library
- Making mail-in comment cards available at the MNWR Headquarters, Chatham Town Hall, and Chatham Public Library
- Posting meeting announcements in local newspapers
- Creating a special project email address to receive comments and questions

The information gathered through these efforts informed the many transportation interventions and several scenarios discussed in Chapters 5 and 6. The public comments complemented expert opinion, data analysis, and discussions with key project partners. Meeting notes and copies of the handouts and information sheets are provided in APPENDIX B.

3.1. General Public

The project team held a public meeting on August 24, 2008, to provide information about the project and solicit feedback. Twenty-two attendees represented (1) the general public and (2) stakeholder/residents groups for the Morris Island and Stage Island neighborhoods that abut MNWR, and (3) elected officials, town and regional government staff. Local media also covered the meeting. After a brief presentation on the project background and goals, participants were asked to discuss major transportation and traffic concerns related to the refuge and potential solutions. A summary of the comments is provided below.

Concerns

Concerns focused on the number of cars accessing Morris Island and the need for options to access both Morris Island and the Monomoy Islands by other (non-vehicular) modes of transportation. Other concerns included access for school groups (and school buses) and the limited handicapped accessibility around Morris Island and to the ferry docks.

While most of the meeting focused on MNWR, there was also some discussion of traffic and parking issues relating to Lighthouse Beach and Bridge Street. Attendees cited the narrow roadway width and parking on both sides of the street as primary concerns.

Attendees raised other important topics, including the seasonal fluctuation of traffic and parking congestion in Chatham. It was recommended that the study team consider transportation-related solutions that are seasonal or are implemented in such a way that is appropriate year-round. Similarly, visitation to the refuge and to the town of Chatham can vary from year to year, depending on various economic or environmental conditions that impact tourism. This study is intended to address both current and future needs of the refuge.

Some participants were concerned that improving information about, and access to, MNWR would increase traffic congestion; it is important to couple activities designed to increase visitation with specific alternative transportation measures that can offset issues.

Solutions

The meeting included a brainstorming session on potential transportation-related solutions to address the concerns summarized above. Many of the solutions suggested by the meeting participants were explored for implementation and are included in the scenarios discussed in Chapter 6. The full list of suggested solutions from the meeting is provided in APPENDIX B.

3.2. Civic and Business Community

A member of the study team was a special guest at a meeting of the Chatham-Orleans Rotary Club on January 14, 2009. The purpose of the meeting was to provide an overview of the study, discuss findings from the existing conditions analysis (conducted in Fall 2008), and solicit feedback about problems and solutions.

Approximately 30 members of the Chatham-Orleans Rotary Club attended the meeting along with an FWS representative. Rotary Club members were familiar with MNWR, but not all participants were residents of the town of Chatham.

Concerns

The group was primarily concerned with vehicular traffic congestion and parking limitations, and their impact on tourism and economic activity in the Chatham area.

Additionally, participants discussed the timing of the study, namely the severity of the transportation issues (such as congestion) in the immediate vicinity of MNWR. The study lead discussed the importance of evaluating and selecting transportation alternatives for implementation before congestion issues reach a "crisis" point. Environmental factors (such as storm effects on erosion and the changing landform) can create serious access and transportation issues in a short period of time. This situation requires MNWR and Chatham-area planners to consider transportation alternatives in the near term.

Solutions

Rotary Club members recommended non-vehicular forms of access, including bicycle and pedestrian facilities on Morris Island and nearby to the refuge. Meeting attendees also recommended that the study team reach out to stakeholder groups engaged in specific hobbies, such as bird-watching and nature photography, in order to solicit additional feedback.

3.3. Written Public Comments

Several avenues were made available for the public to submit written comments to the project team regarding transportation and access to MNWR. These included a project email address and paper comment cards made available at MNWR Headquarters, the Chatham Town Library, and Chatham Town Hall. The study team did not receive any transportation-related concerns, opinions, or suggestions through these means.

3.4. Targeted Stakeholders

On December 18, 2009, the project team held a working session with selected stakeholders and potential partners for implementation activities related the MNWR Alternative Transportation Study. Representatives from FWS, the Chatham Planning Department, the Chatham Department of Public Works, the Cape Cod Commission, and the Chatham Chamber of Commerce attended the working session.

During the working session, the project team and FWS provided the group with information on the study, obtained initial feedback on the identified interventions, and began to discuss the potential for partnering activities to implement various interventions.

Overall, the discussion and the feedback provided during the working meeting were positive. The Town and the Chamber of Commerce both expressed interest in several of the interventions, and identified potential partnership activities. Areas that seemed most ripe for partnership included information and signage improvements and a downtown storefront visitor contact station. The Cape Cod Commission provided insight and comments on several of the interventions, and valuable information about funding opportunities. More detailed notes from the stakeholder meeting are provided in APPENDIX K.

4. PARTNERSHIPS

This study presents a suite of alternative transportation scenarios for FWS to consider implementing in order to achieve transportation goals. Some interventions may be implemented more quickly or effectively in partnership with stakeholders. The purpose of the partnership assessment is to document and assess existing partnerships between MNWR and other stakeholders, and to explore opportunities to develop new partnerships related to transportation and refuge access.

FWS has identified goals related to visitor experience, conservation, and mobility that are consistent with the goals of a variety of local, regional, State, and Federal government entities and civic groups on Cape Cod. FWS has an opportunity to work with these groups to implement specific projects and activities, and develop an ongoing dialogue to achieve long-term success. The partnership assessment is a useful tool for current and future FWS staff. It is important to note that this analysis is transportation focused; suggestions for partnerships relate to access, mobility, wayfinding, and other transportation issues. There are many other existing and potential partnerships related to conservation, biology, ecology, education, and other important issues.

4.1. Partnership Assessment Process

The study team conducted the partnership assessment in three steps: (1) potential partner identification, (2) research and information gathering, and (3) analysis.

Identification of Potential Partners

In order to identify potential partners, the Volpe Center project team developed a broad list of existing local government departments, civic groups, and organizations in the greater Chatham area. The Volpe Center and MNWR staff discussed existing relationships with entities on this list, in order to establish the current partnership conditions and consider ways to strengthen or expand upon existing partnerships. This discussion also led to the identification of potential new partners, as well as groups that would not be likely or strong partners.

The project team then developed a matrix to document each relationship, future possibilities related to the transportation goals and benefits (as well as potential sensitivities or limitations), and whether the partnership would be short- or long-term. The matrix includes a rating (low/medium/high) of the strength of each potential partnership, based on the evaluation of these factors. The potential partners that were rated as either "medium" or "high" were then considered in more detail and are discussed below. The full partnership matrix is available in APPENDIX C.

Research and Information Gathering

The project team gathered additional information about potential partners from existing reports, web sites, and other literature. These findings were used to identify possible activities for each partnership, including initiatives and projects that could be implemented by MNWR and those that could be implemented by the partner.

After confirming the updated partnership matrix with MNWR staff, the project team prepared discussion guidelines and conducted a series of telephone conversations with selected agencies and individuals, in order to better understand potential for initiating or expanding partnerships. Each telephone conversation lasted approximately 30 minutes (when the partner was reached by phone), and findings were documented for analysis.

Analysis

The analysis synthesizes the findings about each of the potential partners and provides recommendations for next steps, if any. The discussion of the potential alternative transportation scenarios identified the key partnerships necessary to ensure the success of each suggested transportation intervention.

This partnership assessment is intended to assist FWS in making informed decisions about the organizations that could work with MNWR toward achieving many of the goals outlined in this study. This assessment outlines the nature of each potential partnership, potential activities, and the transportation interventions that could be implemented or strengthened by leveraging a partnership.

Regional Agencies and Organizations

Cape Cod Commission

The Cape Cod Commission (CCC) is the regional land use and transportation planning agency for Barnstable County. The CCC and MNWR worked together to prepare the application for this alternative transportation study, and to gather and supply data for the study. As part of future partner activities, CCC could provide traffic counting data, assist in planning and developing alternative transportation projects within the metropolitan transportation planning process, and act as a liaison with the Cape Cod Regional Transit Authority (CCRTA). In return, MNWR could seek funding for joint capital projects, such as shuttle vehicles, and provide relevant transportation data about refuge visitors.

CCC has indicated that it would be very interested in partnering with MNWR to achieve mutual goals that include improving alternative transportation access throughout Cape Cod. Partnering with the CCC will be key to implementing portions of all four alternative transportation scenarios. Specifically, this relationship could be valuable in implementing interventions related to shuttle service, signage, and wayfinding.

Cape Cod Regional Transit Authority

The Cape Cod Regional Transit Authority (CCRTA) is the regional transit agency that serves Cape Cod. While the CCRTA and MNWR currently have no existing relationship, a partnership could be advantageous if FWS decides to pursue shuttle or other transit service to MNWR, as described in Scenario 1.

While CCRTA has indicated that it is not currently in a position to initiate new service in Chatham, there is some limited potential for a future arrangement. Under such an arrangement, MNWR might seek Federal Transit Administration funds for capital expenses such as vehicles and transit stop amenities (e.g., bus shelters, benches, etc.). In the nearer term if FWS decides to pursue a shuttle to MNWR, coordination with CCRTA would be important for providing connections between the regional and local services, and announcing and promoting the new service to riders.

Town of Chatham Departments

The town of Chatham would be a critical partner for MNWR to implement nearly any alternative transportation improvements.

Chatham Public Schools

At present, the Chatham Public Schools and MNWR have an education-based relationship; individual teachers request field trips to the refuge, while MNWR provides tours and interpretive information. As part of an expanded partnership, Chatham Public Schools could allow the refuge to use existing surface lots for a satellite parking facility and hub for a refuge shuttle. In turn, pending additional staffing, MNWR could explore the possibility of establishing a formal environmental educational relationship with the schools.

Chatham Public Schools would be a critical partner in the implementation of Scenario 1, which proposes use of the Chatham Jr/Sr High School and/or Chatham Elementary School parking lots, during the summer and on seasonal weekends for satellite parking for a shuttle service.

The project team has not been successful in discussing the potential for such a partnership with the Chatham School Department. Because of this, it is difficult at this point to characterize their level of interest or the administrative steps necessary to implement such an arrangement. It is also important to note that initiating such an arrangement may take some time and require extensive discussions, as it is new territory for both MNWR and the School Department. A transportation partnership with MNWR is not likely to be high among the School Department priorities; this will affect the speed with which discussions may take place. Still, it may be possible to discuss a pilot arrangement for the 2011 season, with limited parking in school lots available in June, July, and August 2011.

Chatham Planning Department

The existing relationship between the Planning Department and MNWR so far has focused on preparing for and conducting this alternative transportation study. The project team has worked closely with the Planning

Department to ensure that the alternative transportation scenarios could be feasible in the current planning and political climate.

The Planning Department has indicated interest in continuing and possibly expanding upon the existing relationship with MNWR. As part of an expanded partnership, the Planning Department could support MNWR's efforts to provide alternative methods to access to the refuge by helping to identify satellite parking locations, facilitate improvements, and assist in updating signage. Such a partnership could prove beneficial for the town as well, as many of the possible improvements to MNWR access could also provide more general transportation and access improvements throughout Chatham. One contribution of FWS to such a partnership is access to Federal grant programs that could provide funding for some projects that would support transportation-related goals of both the refuge and the town.

A partnership with the Chatham Planning Department will be critical to the implementation of all identified scenarios; the Planning Department has the greatest local expertise and ability to help implement alternative transportation interventions involving transit, signage, bicycle and pedestrian improvements, visitor contact station relocation, water based access improvements, and minor road projects.

Chatham Public Works Department
MNWR currently has a limited relationship with the Public Works Department (DPW) of the town of Chatham. The DPW is responsible for roadway and public right of way maintenance, and would be a necessary partner for any interventions related to roadway improvements, sidewalks, or signage. Potential partnership opportunities with the DPW could be surrounding the maintenance of the bicycle information kiosks, and increasing communication about upcoming and planned projects.

Chatham Police Department
The existing relationship between the Police Department and MNWR is limited; presently the Police Department helps to direct lost travelers looking for the refuge, and aides MNWR when it finds historic human remains on-site. The Chatham Police Department provides valuable data about traffic violations and accidents in Chatham and on roadways nearby to the refuge. In the future, MNWR hopes that the Police Department will continue to aid the refuge in these ways.

Chatham Landing Officer
Presently the Town Landing Officer and MNWR have a limited relationship. A more formal relationship could facilitate further cooperation on coastal and water-based access issues.

Chatham Bikeways Committee
The Chatham Bikeways Committee is composed of volunteer residents with interest and experience in nonmotorized transportation and cycling. The committee meets regularly and serves the town in an advisory capacity. Committee members do not have set terms, but serve on the committee until their work is completed. The committee has a Board of Selectmen liaison, as well as liaisons in the planning and public works departments. MNWR and the Bikeways Committee have no existing relationship. If a partnership were

established, the Bikeways Committee might be able to provide support to MNWR on improvements to bicycle access, such as maps, signage, parking, and publicity. A specific project that might benefit from collaboration would be improvements to existing or sponsorship of new bicycle kiosks. Such improvements, while targeted at MNWR, could enhance bicycling conditions throughout Chatham. MNWR may be able to provide funding (either through its own budget or apply for grants) to support such efforts.

A relationship with the Bikeways Committee could support implementation of all of the scenarios, particularly those with specific bicycle improvements, highlighted in Scenarios 1, 3, and 4.

Massachusetts State Agencies

Massachusetts Department of Conservation and Recreation (DCR)
DCR is the State agency that maintains 450,000 acres of State-owned natural and recreational resources. While DCR and MNWR do not have an existing relationship, DCR has expressed a high level of interest in establishing a partnership. Specific areas of interest include marketing assets and attractions on the DCR bike trails, namely the Cape Cod Rail Trail (CCRT) and its Chatham branch extension. DCR would have no formal barriers or constraints to such a partnership, and would be interested in further discussion with MNWR.

A partnership with DCR will be important in all scenarios, specifically for interventions that deal with signage solutions throughout Cape Cod and along Route 6.

Massachusetts Department of Transportation
The Massachusetts Department of Transportation (MassDOT) is the primary surface transportation agency for the Commonwealth of Massachusetts, responsible for all State and Interstate highways, excluding the Massachusetts Turnpike. Presently, the MassDOT has no relationship with MNWR.

MassDOT will be an important partner for implementing several of the alternative transportation interventions proposed in this report, particularly those that include roadway improvements on State-maintained roads. There is potential for partnership on all proposed scenarios, MassDOT could support MNWR in signage projects and in the implementation of pedestrian and bicycle improvements.

U.S. Federal Agencies

U.S. Fish and Wildlife Service (USFWS), Region 5
The FWS Regional Refuge Roads Program Manager works out of the Regional Office in Hadley, Massachusetts and can support and help secure funding for improvements and maintenance services.

National Park Service, Cape Cod National Seashore (CACO)

As the manager of the Cape Cod coastline, CACO has worked extensively with MNWR, jointly planning to map the coastline, and creating timelines for changing land masses; in addition CACO performs prescribed burning in the area. Under an expanded partnership, CACO and MNWR could collaborate to improve alternative transportation options to both MNWR and to Lighthouse Beach.

Partnership with CACO could be helpful in implementing interventions related to providing enhanced bicycle and pedestrian facilities at the headquarters/visitor contact station, Lighthouse Beach and throughout the downtown, as proposed in Scenarios 4 and 5.

U.S. Coast Guard (USCG), Chatham Harbor Master
Presently, the USCG and the Chatham Harbor Master work with MNWR to recover lost or stuck boaters. It will be important to maintain this relationship, especially if additional waterfront access to MNWR becomes available.

Transportation Service Partners

Monomoy Island Ferry (Rip Ryder)
Rip Ryder is one of two ferry concessionaires authorized to land on the Monomoy Islands. Passengers currently park in the lot at the headquarters/visitor contact station and the boat disembarks from the bottom of the stairs at Morris Island. If MNWR were to relocate the visitor contact station or acquire an alternate dock space, the partnership with Rip Ryder could be expanded to include transporting passengers between parking and dock areas. Under an expanded concession agreement, Rip Ryder could enhance its services, such as providing rental of canoe/kayak or fishing equipment.

Outermost Harbor Marine
Outermost Harbor Marine is one of two ferry concessionaires authorized to land on the Monomoy Islands. Presently passengers park at and the ferry leaves from Outermost Harbor Marine. If MNWR were to relocate the visitor contact station or acquire an alternate dock space, the partnership with Outermost Harbor Marine could be expanded to include transporting passengers between parking and dock areas. Under an expanded concession agreement, Outermost Harbor Marine could enhance its services, such as providing rental of canoe/kayak or fishing equipment.

Local Media, Civic, and Business Associations

Cape Code Chronicle, Cape Cod Times, and Radio WQRC
These local media outlets presently promote and provide information about events and happenings at MNWR. If the relationship with any of these entities was expanded, each could provide up to date information on transportation issues, such as closed roads or upcoming issues with shuttle service.

Chatham Chamber of Commerce

The Chatham Chamber of Commerce (Chamber) and MNWR have historically had a minimal relationship, with the Chamber passing out MNWR materials. However, under new leadership, the Chamber expressed interest in partnering with MNWR in any feasible way. An expanded partnership through a downtown or West Chatham Village visitor contact station is of particular interest, though the Chamber is open to additional partnering possibilities.

The Chamber could be an important partner in providing pedestrian and bicycle amenities downtown, such as at shuttle stops as proposed in Scenario 1 or at a downtown visitor contact station, as proposed in Scenario 2.

Chatham Council on Aging

MNWR and the Chatham Council on Aging (Council) have no existing relationship. One possibility is that MNWR and the Council could partner through promoting senior usage of and access to MNWR, including the possibility of Council transportation to the refuge. The project team has not been successful in discussing a potential partnership with the Council. Because of this, it is difficult at this point to characterize their level of interest or the necessary administrative steps to implement such an arrangement. It is also important to note that initiating such an arrangement may take some time and require extensive discussions, as it is new territory for both MNWR and the Council.

Chatham Historical Society

In the present partnership between MNWR and the Chatham Historical Society, MNWR has provided presentations at the Chatham Historical Society, and the Historical Society has performed research on the history of MNWR. The Chatham Historical Society could continue to perform research, as well as promote alternative transportation options to MNWR.

Mass Audubon – Wellfleet Bay Wildlife Sanctuary

The Wellfleet Bay Wildlife Sanctuary holds birding walks at MNWR one to two times per week, using the Outermost Harbor Marine ferry to reach the islands. The current relationship is based on outreach and providing the public with a hands on wildlife experience. In the future, the Wellfleet Bay Wildlife Sanctuary could provide information on and promote use of alternative transportation options.

Mass Audubon – Coastal Waterbird

Presently the relationship between MNWR and Mass Audubon-Coastal Waterbird is primarily research-based; Mass Audubon researchers stay in the field camp on the Monomoy Islands and the two organizations partner on surveys. If the partnership were enhanced, Mass Audubon- Coastal Waterbird could explore how transportation improvements would impact sensitive species. The groups could also continue to collaborate on species research.

4.2. Findings and Recommendations

All of the proposed alternative transportation scenarios could be significantly enhanced if MNWR formed partnerships with other local, regional, State and Federal entities. Partnering can ease MNWR's financial burden for suggested interventions and increase political palatability, therefore reducing controversy associated with any of the potential alterative transportation interventions.

Although certain entities have more to gain from partnering with MNWR, there seems to be a general enthusiasm for working with MNWR to undertake mutually beneficial activities. MNWR should capitalize upon this willingness to partner when moving forward with any transportation intervention. In particular, MNWR may want to focus on working with groups that have a significant stake in Chatham, and genuinely wish to enhance the community, and access to its resources.

This study focuses on partnerships that will best foster or improve alternative transportation and access to MNWR. It is important to note that this is only one type of partnership that could exist between MNWR and other organizations. Moving forward, MNWR should consider which types of partnerships it hopes to access, and pursue those that can help achieve mutual goals.

5. TRANSPORTATION INTERVENTIONS

This alternative transportation study is founded upon a careful review of existing conditions (including planning documents and policy statements), public input, and information from key stakeholders. The study team used this analysis to identify a series of transportation "interventions" – these can be solutions to problems, opportunities, specific projects or initiatives. Interventions can focus on engineering, travel behavior, or traveler information (and others).

The interventions described in this section are the building blocks of the scenarios presented in the next chapter. Each intervention is described in terms of its components or elements, costs, objectives, and relevance for MNWR and Chatham, MA. To the extent possible, the study team has tried to include visual aids (maps, photos, drawings) that represent real-world examples of interventions. Some of these interventions are featured throughout several of the scenarios; others may appear in only one.

The study team expects each intervention to help achieve at least one (but in most cases several) of the following outcomes:

- Reduce traffic congestion (generally in the Chatham area, and specifically around the MNWR headquarters/visitor contact station);
- Improve traffic flow (generally in the Chatham area, and specifically around the MNWR headquarters/visitor contact station);
- Expand parking options for MNWR visitors and seasonal travelers;
- Expand public transit options (to the MNWR headquarters/visitor contact station, and more generally in the Chatham area);
- Facilitate travel by bicycle and walking (generally in the Chatham area, but also to the MNWR headquarters/visitor contact station);
- Reduce confusion or lack of knowledge about travel options in and around MNWR; and
- Leverage partnerships and improve relationships among transportation stakeholders in the Chatham area.

Interventions must be *evaluated* and *described*. The next section provides a descriptive overview of each intervention. The process of evaluating individual interventions against criteria such as cost, technical difficulty, or political support helped the study team move forward to assemble the scenarios.

5.1. Evaluating the Interventions

The evaluation approach was designed to allow FWS to understand the feasibility of implementing each individual intervention, as well as combinations of interventions (a scenario), to adequately meet multiple project goals. This approach is predicated on the understanding that some interventions are most effective when implemented in combination with other interventions. For example, creating a satellite parking facility several miles away from the refuge will likely be successful only if shuttle service is also provided. These interventions go hand-in-hand to address the project goals. The study team has taken a high-level, strategic approach to developing the scenarios, creating combinations of actions designed to achieve maximum success.

The study team considered a broad list of 39 potential transportation interventions to address local transportation issues and meet project goals. The study team developed a set of criteria in consultation with FWS staff and then rated each of the interventions based on the following criteria:

- Cost
- Level of difficulty to implement (Technical / Engineering)
- Political sensitivity
- Environmental constraints or limitations
- Impact on habitat protection
- Public approval or support
- Impact on refuge visitation
- Implementation time frame (within one fiscal year, 1-2 years, 2-5 years, 5+ years)
- FWS ability to implement; and
- Need for partnership to implement.

The analysis includes a rating of low/medium/high for most of the criteria, with other descriptions and comments provided as necessary. Based on this initial assessment, the list of interventions was narrowed to 21 "high" feasibility options, which were then researched in greater detail to determine how they could be implemented by MNWR and to estimate costs.

The full list of interventions, with the preliminary assessment and related comments, is provided in APPENDIX D.

5.2. Describing the Interventions

The interventions described below are grouped into five categories, and include:

Multimodal Roadway/Sidewalk Engineering Improvements
1. Relocate and reinstall Causeway fencing to better accommodate parked cars and emergency vehicles
2. Create multi-use path on one side of Causeway for bicycles and pedestrians
3. Construct sidewalk between Bridge Street parking areas and Lighthouse Beach
4. Paint "sharrow" or shared lane markings on signed bicycle route
5. Provide bicycle facilities and amenities at shuttle stops
6. Provide pedestrian improvements at and around shuttle stops
7. Add bicycle and pedestrian facilities and enhanced amenities at new visitor contact station
8. Provide additional bicycle racks at MNWR headquarters/visitor contact station, Lighthouse Beach, and high priority downtown locations

Vehicular Parking Interventions
9. Identify/secure satellite parking location
10. Implement parking restrictions at MNWR headquarters/visitor contact station

Transit Service
11. Operate shuttle service to MNWR (and other destinations in Chatham) from satellite parking
12. Contract with taxi service or other provider to offer demand responsive, shared taxi service to MNWR (and other destinations in Chatham) from satellite parking
13. Provide a multi-passenger shuttle from a new downtown visitor contact station to Morris Island

Signage, Wayfinding, and Information
14. Use variable message signs at new/redesigned intersection to direct visitors to satellite parking
15. Improve bicycle route signage
16. Improve directional signage to MNWR headquarters/visitor contact station
17. Add directional and informational signage throughout Chatham
18. Add directional and information signage throughout Cape Cod and along Route 6
19. Improve traveler information on MNWR website

Other
20. Relocate MNWR visitor contact station
21. Improve waterfront access

Multimodal Roadway/Sidewalk Engineering Improvements

This category includes interventions that address engineering, road geometry, sidewalk facilities, and similar. These interventions address multiple travel modes: vehicular, pedestrian, and cycling.

1.   Relocate and reinstall Causeway fencing to better accommodate parked cars and emergency vehicles

The town of Chatham owns the section of Morris Island Road that connects the mainland to Morris Island, known as "the Causeway." This section of roadway has two relatively narrow travel lanes; parking for shellfishers, kayakers, and MNWR visitors is permitted on one side of the road, which effectively narrows the travel area by 4-6 feet. The road's right-of-way includes an additional ~14 feet of unpaved area that could be utilized to relieve parking or travel pressure.

Although there is sufficient right-of-way to add another lane for travel or parking on the Causeway, historically the town has not wanted to pursue this option due to opposition from local residents related to perceived increases in traffic congestion. An alternative is to relocate and reinstall the existing fencing to provide more space for parked cars. Although the area would not be paved, it would allow more space for cars to pull out of the travel lane when parking. This would improve Causeway safety and also allow more space for emergency vehicles to travel across the Causeway even when vehicles are parked there.

Based on shared anecdotal information about the condition and age of the fencing, FWS staff believes that the fencing will need to be replaced by the town within five years of completion of this study. This situation may provide a good opportunity to move the fencing to allow more width for parking. While the parking area would not be paved, it would be wise to use crushed stone or a similar material to help stabilize the surface and prevent erosion. Because the Causeway is built on dredge spoil, serious wetland or other environmental issues are not anticipated.

Removing the existing fencing and planning, designing, and construction for a 10-foot crushed stone parking area and new fencing is expected to cost approximately $125,000. The stone would likely have to be replaced every year or two, which would cost approximately $5,000 for each replacement, not including labor.

2.   Create multi-use path on one side of Causeway for bicycles and pedestrians

There is sufficient right-of-way for the town of Chatham to repurpose some currently unpaved areas for a dedicated bicycle and pedestrian path in order to improve safety and attractiveness of bicycling or walking on the narrow and crowded road. The path could be paved with asphalt or concrete, or constructed with a "soft surface" such as crushed stone. A crushed stone path (3/8" crusher fines or less) can provide a smooth and accessible surface for bicyclists and pedestrians. A soft surface path might be preferable to maintain the natural character of the environment. They are typically less expensive to build, but can increase the maintenance burden, depending on weather and choice of material. It might also be possible to use colored asphalt or concrete, as a way to maintain a more rural appearance.

Additional safety features, such as a crosswalk or flashing light at the beginning of the Causeway might be appropriate, to assist users of the path in transitioning from mixed traffic on Morris Island Road to the path.

Removing the existing fencing, planning, designing, and construction for an 8-foot crushed stone multi-use path and new fencing is expected to cost approximately $85,000. Maintenance costs are expected to be approximately $1-2,000 per year. Because the Causeway is built on dredge spoil, serious wetland or other environmental issues are not anticipated.

3.   Construct sidewalk between Bridge Street parking areas and Lighthouse Beach

Providing a sidewalk on the portion of Bridge Street and Main Street between the parking area and Lighthouse Beach could improve safety and reduce potential for conflicts between pedestrians and motorists. Initial estimates indicate that the section of roadway without adequate sidewalks is approximately 0.5 miles in length.

There may be sufficient right of way to construct sidewalks on at least one side of the portions of Main Street and Bridge Street that connect the Lighthouse and the Bridge Street parking area. While the right of way does exist, it may appear to be part of individual front lawns, which could make such construction politically unpopular. Alternately, if beach-goers currently walk in front lawns to access the beach, then provision of sidewalks could be more popular. It will be important to confirm that there is sufficient width to allow for both a sidewalk and the beach parking itself.

Curbing and sidewalk construction for about half a mile (on one side of the street) would cost in the range of $200,000.

4.   Paint "sharrow" or shared lane markings on signed bicycle route

One option for improving bicycle access throughout Chatham and to MNWR is to paint shared lane markings, or "sharrows" on the signed bicycle routes. These markings indicate that the lane is intended to be shared by automobiles and bicycles. Painting such markings would serve two purposes – it would clearly indicate and remind drivers of the presence of cyclists, and it would also direct cyclists to the recommended route. An example of such a marking is shown below.

The actual painting of the symbols or roadway markings can be implemented relatively quickly, with the greatest amount of time spent determining which streets need markings and what type of markings to use. This process would need to be coordinated with the town of Chatham, the Cape Cod Commission, and the MassDOT Highway Department. The existing bicycle route includes several junctions with local roads; these junctions should be top priorities for adding pavement markings, and are identified on the attached map.

It should be noted that sharrows are typically painted on wide outside lanes of 12 to 14 feet, multi-lane roads. The roadways on the signed bicycle route primarily have only one travel lane in each direction, and the travel lanes are narrower. Further discussions with the MassDOT Highway Department are recommended to determine whether these roadways are appropriate for sharrow markings.

Depending on the size and type of marking used, sharrow markings can cost $50-100 per symbol. Sharrow markings at intervals of approximately every 250 feet (and at key intersections) would cost in the range of $10-15,000.

5.   Provide bicycle facilities and amenities with shuttle service

Providing bicycle facilities and amenities with shuttle service could increase ridership and improve connectivity between the shuttle service and bicycle routes to and from MNWR and other major Chatham attractions. Shuttle stops could feature bicycle racks, shelters, trash cans, and traveler information kiosks/boards.

Source: Joseph Bellomo Architects

One option is to provide bicycle racks on the shuttle vehicles. A variety of transit vehicles can be equipped with racks to hold bicycles on the front of the back of the vehicle. The most common style of rack is mounted in front, and holds two bicycles. A front mounted rack is typically considered preferable because it allows passengers to see the bicycles and ensure that they are not removed or damaged at interim stops. In addition, a front mounted rack allows the driver to see that passengers are loading or unloading their bicycles. Rear mounted racks are also available, if there is a need for either a rear rack or enough demand for both a front and rear rack. Another option in areas with high demand for bicycles on buses is to use a bicycle trailer. Trailers are hitched to the back of the vehicle and typically hold 12-16 bicycles.

If using a rear rack or trailer, an additional mirror in the vehicle is recommended for safety. Bicycle racks for buses are also able to fit on smaller vehicles, as small as a 14-passenger cut-away van.

Source: Dan Burden

Depending on the type of vehicle and connection, front mounted bicycle racks cost in the range of $500-1,000 per rack. Trailers cost in the range of $10,000-15,000.

6.   Provide pedestrian improvements at and around shuttle stops

Pedestrians must be able to safely and comfortably access the shuttle stops. Appropriate improvements include: sidewalk construction, painted crosswalks, crossing signals with countdown, pedestrian crosswalk cones, and ADA-accessible ramps and markings at intersections. Other pedestrian improvements include shelters, benches, trash cans, and traveler information kiosks/boards.

7.   Add bicycle and pedestrian facilities and enhanced amenities at new Visitor Contact Station

A downtown MNWR visitor contact station (purchased as-is or new construction) should include bicycle and pedestrian facilities and amenities. Presently, the town of Chatham and MNWR provide basic bicycle and pedestrian services. Improving these services and clustering facilities in a central location might encourage more visitors to ride a bicycle or walk to MNWR. Providing additional amenities would not only make MNWR a destination for visitors who favor bicycle or pedestrian travel, but also provide recreational and transportation options to the greater Chatham community.

Bicycle and pedestrian amenities might include:
- Bicycle racks
- Shelters
- Essential bicycle repair tools
- Showers for cyclists
- Benches
- Water fountains
- Garbage cans

These amenities could make bicyclists and pedestrians feel more comfortable and make the new visitor contact station a destination. Adding these types of amenities could also improve safety for bicyclists and provide resting places for pedestrians.

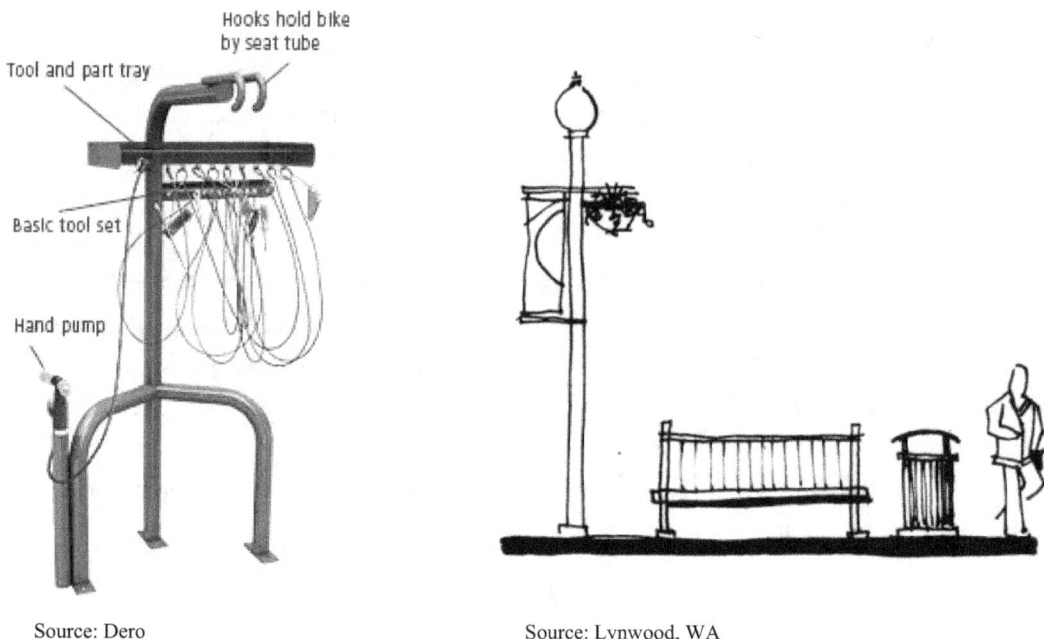

Source: Dero   Source: Lynwood, WA

8.   Provide additional bicycle racks at Visitor Contact Station, Lighthouse Beach, and high priority downtown locations

Modern bicycle racks provide a safe and secure place to park and store bicycles at visitor destinations. There are currently some racks at the MNWR headquarters/visitor contact station and Lighthouse Beach, but provision of additional racks could encourage increased visitation via bicycle.

Bicycle rack installation requires a relatively flat, clear surface with adequate clearance space to allow for movement around the bicycles. Racks can range from holding two bicycles to more than ten each, and are available in a variety of styles and shapes.

Standard hoop and rolling racks cost approximately $80-100 per bicycle, with more artistic and custom designs costing more. Space requirements vary depending on the size and shape of the rack.

Traditional "hoop" rack with handlebar embellishment.
Source http://esterofl.org/

Traditional "rolling" rack.
Source: The Presidio Trust

Vehicular Parking Interventions

9.   Identify/secure a satellite parking location

Through discussions with the Chatham Planning Department, the Chatham Jr/Sr High School and Chatham Elementary School have been identified as a potentially viable location for alternate parking facilities. The public parking areas in and around the downtown are stressed during the summer, making them unavailable to provide extra capacity for visitors to MNWR or to Lighthouse Beach. A satellite parking location should have sufficient capacity to provide relief to downtown drivers and visitors to MNWR or Lighthouse Beach.

Satellite parking and shuttle service would be available during peak summer tourist season, which typically runs from Memorial Day to Labor Day. Weekend visitation remains high through September and usually until Columbus Day. Ideally, satellite parking would be available every day during peak season and on weekends during the "shoulder season," from Labor Day to Columbus Day. Use of school parking lots for summer tourist parking is constrained by the academic calendar. The Chatham School Department calendar for the 2009-2010 school year runs from Thursday, September 3rd (before Labor Day) to June 29th (assuming five snow days). If school lots are to be used, then they would only be available on weekends while school is in session, thus shortening the shuttle season by as much as eight weeks.

It should be noted that the high school is not in walking distance to the downtown area or to Morris Island. The elementary school is located near the end of the Chatham Extension of the Cape Cod Rail Trail, and is about a half mile from the "top" of Main Street in Downtown Chatham. Depending on a visitor's desired destinations, it could be a reasonable (although somewhat long) walk to Downtown Chatham, but it is not in walking distance to Morris Island. Using either of these locations as alternate parking for Lighthouse Beach or Morris Island would require use of shuttle or transit service. The two locations are shown in Map 10.

Map 10: Potential Satellite Parking Locations

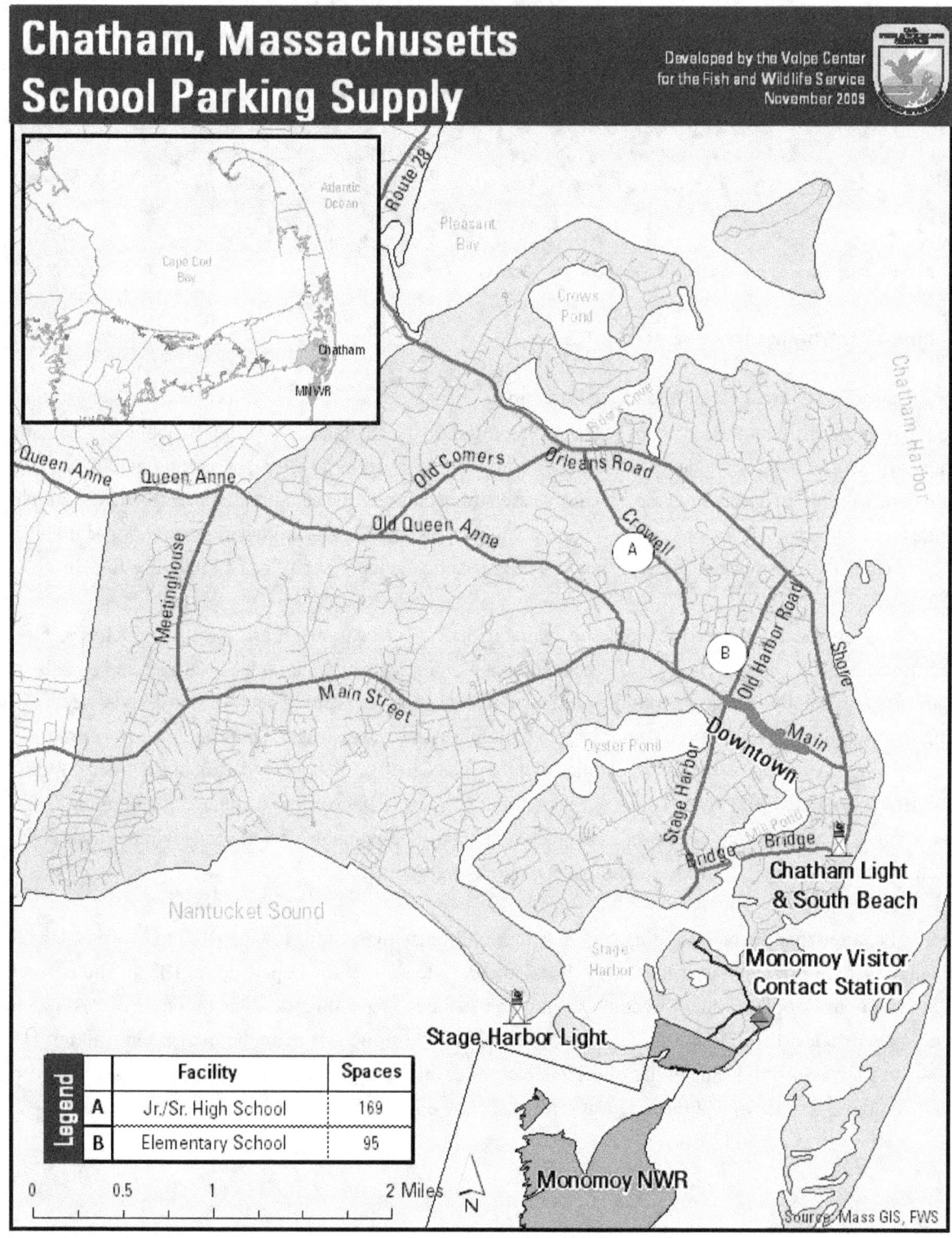

10.   Implement Parking Restrictions at MNWR Headquarters/Visitor Contact Station

Implementing and enforcing parking restrictions at the MNWR headquarters/visitor contact station could meet a variety of objectives, such as discouraging inappropriate use of the parking lot and encouraging use of any new shuttle services. The two primary parking restrictions are (1) a parking fee or (2) an enforced time limit for parking in the lot. Both interventions would discourage non-MNWR use of the parking lot, and help to ensure that spaces are available for visitors to MNWR.

1.   Charge a nominal fee for use of the MNWR Headquarters/Visitor Contact Station Parking Lot

In 2004, Congress passed the Federal Lands Recreation Enhancement Act, allowing the Federal government to charge a fee for the recreational use of public lands. Nationally, 112 FWS refuges charge a recreational fee for certain uses at each refuge. These fees can include a hunt fee, boat launch fee, annual pass or entrance fee. At least 80 percent of the fees collected are reinvested into the refuge and 20 percent are used in the geographic region.

One Massachusetts refuge that charges an entrance fee is the Parker River NWR; other refuges may elect to charge a fee in the future. Parker River NWR charges a daily entrance fee of $5/car, $2/walk or bicycle or $20 for an annual pass. The fee is only for the Plum Island section of the refuge and is collected at the refuge entrance gatehouse during business hours, and at other times, using an honor system known as the "iron ranger." Collecting an entrance fee for parking at MNWR could deter casual parkers and those not visiting the refuge; it could also generate a small amount of revenue for MNWR to reinvest in other transportation activities at the refuge.

MNWR could implement one of three styles of fee collection for the headquarters/visitor contact station parking lot. The first would be the model used at Parker River, which involves the use of a gatehouse. In order to implement this model, MNWR would need to identify a site for and build the gatehouse, then develop a plan to provide staff for the gatehouse.

The second model would be an automated gate, where the parking vehicle accepts a ticket upon entry. The fee could be paid inside the visitor contact station, and the vehicle would then receive a paid card, to exit the parking lot. This would require full time staffing of the visitor contact station, though the gate could be left open during hours when the visitor contact station is closed. Either of these two models ranges in cost from $5,000-$10,000, not including staffing costs.

The third fee implementation model would require the smallest investment of personnel: paying the fee to an "iron ranger" on the "honor system." While this model is difficult to enforce, it discourages non-paying visitors, and may give the impression that the area is monitored. Original style iron rangers are simply drop bins, however, newer models can print window stickers, permits or receipts.

Source: Mass.gov   http://www.mitico.com/

2. <u>Enforce non-fee time restrictions in the Visitor Contact Station Parking Lot</u>

Non-fee restrictions for the MNWR parking lot would limit the number of hours a vehicle may park in the lot and issue fines for violations.

Prior to implementing this approach, MNWR would need to establish an appropriate parking time limit (for example, one hour, two hours, four hours, etc.) based on the amount of time that visitors need to utilize the resources available at the visitor contact station in order to determine the appropriate parking time limit. This time will determine the allowable parking duration. This system would also require the purchase of several signs that clearly advertise the parking time limitation and consequences of non-compliance.

A critical element of the time based parking restriction would be enforcement of the parking limits. If a visitor parks longer than the posted time, the parking offense is considered trespassing and a fee can be levied by USFWS. In order to enforce the parking limit, MNWR could either hire a law enforcement officer to mark tires and patrol the lot, or MNWR could purchase a camera system to observe the length of time a vehicle is parked in the lot. Each offense would incur a $50 fine, a precedent set by other USFWS refuges that is equal to the fine at Lighthouse Beach in Chatham.

Transit Service

11.   Operate shuttle service to MNWR and throughout Chatham from satellite parking

An independent shuttle system could serve key destinations in Chatham (including MNWR) and also make connections to region-wide Cape Cod transit. The two potential route options discussed below originate at the High School on Crowell Road and serve downtown, Lighthouse Beach, and MNWR. Both routes would also include a transfer point to connect to the existing CCRTA H2O route that serves Chatham. The two routes differ in that the "Loop Route" would travel in only one direction on Main Street, along Stage Harbor Road and could also serve Oyster Pond Beach, whereas the "Linear Route" would travel in both directions on Main Street.

The shuttle route analysis is based on the following assumptions:

- Shuttle service would operate daily from Memorial Day until Labor Day, and on weekends only from Labor Day until Columbus Day;
- Shuttle service would run every 20 minutes from 8:00am to 10:00pm Monday through Saturday, and from 8:00am to 8:00pm on Sunday;

The routes are shown in Map 11. Details of the two routes are provided in Table 12 below, with greater detail provided in APPENDIX E.

Table 12: Potential Shuttle Operations Details

	Loop Route	Linear Route
Round trip distance (miles)	7.7	7.2
Round trip travel time (min)	46	52
Potential stop locations	<ul><li>High School</li><li>Main St. / Depot Road / CVS H2O stop</li><li>Main St. / Stage Harbor Rd.</li><li>Chatham Bars Ave.</li><li>Main St. / Shore Rd.</li><li>Lighthouse Beach</li><li>Morris Island</li><li>Oyster Pond Beach</li><li>Main St. / Depot Rd / CVS H2O stop</li></ul>	<ul><li>High School</li><li>Main St. / Depot Rd. / CVS H2O stop</li><li>Main St. / Stage Harbor Rd.</li><li>Chatham Bars Ave.</li><li>Main St. / Shore Rd.</li><li>Lighthouse Beach</li><li>Morris Island</li></ul>(stops in both direction)
Estimated annual operating costs (three vehicles)	$300,000	$300,000

Preliminary estimates indicate that the cost of operating and maintaining a daily shuttle during the summer peak season would cost approximately $300,000 per season. This would include three vehicles in service at a time. Given the length of the routes and the relatively slow travel speeds through downtown Chatham, three vehicles would be required to maintain service every 20 minutes. This level of service is likely the minimum frequency that could encourage visitors to choose the shuttle instead of driving. It might be preferable to run the service even more frequently, which would require additional vehicles.

Vehicle costs vary widely, depending upon the design and type of vehicle selected. Some open-air hybrid tram vehicles are available for approximately $15,000-30,000, while traditional diesel vehicles (such as small buses) can cost an order of magnitude more -- $150,000 to $300,000.

Map 11: Potential Chatham/MNWR Shuttle Service

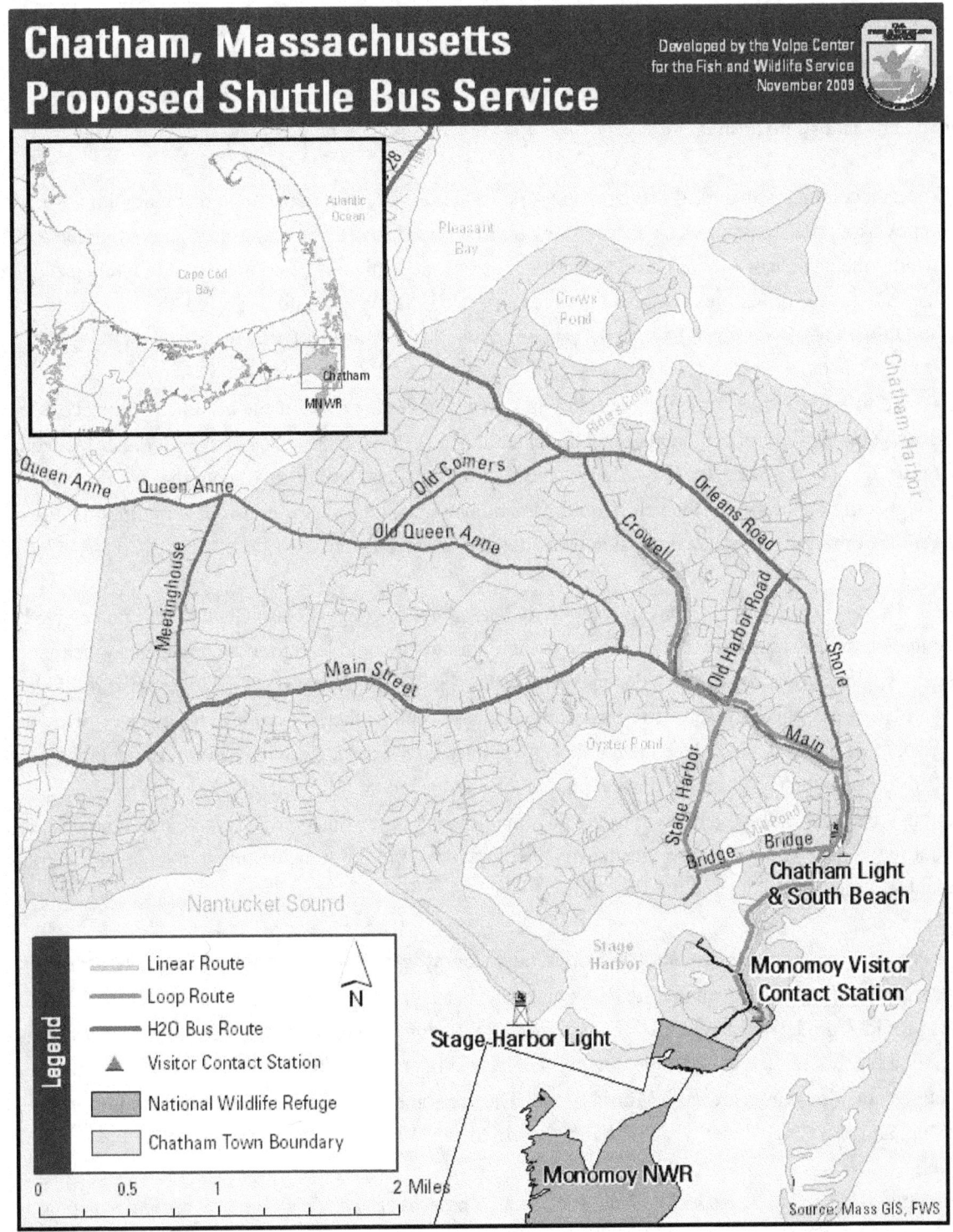

12. Contract with taxi service or other provider to offer demand responsive, shared taxi service to MNWR (and other destinations in Chatham) from satellite parking

One option for providing transit service to MNWR would be to explore the use of a shared use taxi or jitney service. Because of the relatively low cost for vehicles and operations, such a system might be a good way to ease into transit service for MNWR. If it proves to be successful and demand grows, the service could be expanded and made more formal.

MNWR would contract with a local taxi company to provide service, or arrange an agreement with a Friends of Monomoy group to donate services. Depending on the service provider, the contract could either have the driver owning the vehicle or MNWR could purchase or lease the vehicle. The contract would likely provide a base salary rate for the driver plus an agreed upon cost per ride. MNWR would likely pay the salary rate (unless the drivers were volunteers), while the passenger would pay the cost for the ride.

Service could follow a model similar to the following: two vehicles are available at all times of service, with one stationed at a satellite parking facility and the other at MNWR. When a visitor arrives at either location and wants to travel to the other, the driver ferries the visitor to the destination and then returns to the home station. Depending on the size of the vehicle and demand patterns, the driver might wait for additional riders to fill the vehicle, or might drive the visitor as soon as the visitor is ready.

This type of service model may or may not lead to decreased traffic congestion in Chatham if one vehicle load of passengers is simply transported in a different vehicle. In fact, it could lead to more vehicles on the road, because the vehicle would travel to the destination and then back to the home station. However, if multiple vehicles worth of passengers are able to be transported in one vehicle, then it does lead to fewer vehicles on the roads. Also, even if it does not reduce the number of vehicles on the road, it could reduce parking pressure at MNWR (or other potential passenger destinations, if the service would allow them to be taken to other destinations). Because of the relatively low capital and operating costs, this type of service might be desirable as the first step in providing transit service to MNWR, with the option of transitioning to a more formal transit service in the future if demand and funding allow.

13.   Provide a multi-passenger shuttle from a new Downtown Visitor Contact Station to Morris Island

A round trip shuttle service traveling directly from a downtown visitor contact station to Morris Island would either be provided directly by FWS or by a concessionaire, such as one of the Monomoy Island ferry operators. The benefit of such a service would be to directly deliver visitors to MNWR attractions, reducing traffic in areas between the downtown area and Morris Island. The convenience of this shuttle could also improve visitor-ship, and encourage casual visitors to make a trip to MNWR.

This shuttle would need to be a small vehicle, such as a 15 passenger van. This type of vehicle costs roughly $50,000 to purchase. During non-operational hours, the shuttle vehicle could be stored at the new MNWR visitor contact station or at headquarters on Morris Island

Signage, Wayfinding, and Information

Improving signage and wayfinding has been shown to be an effective strategy for reducing visitor or traveler confusion, and expanding access to key destinations. In some cases, improved signage can also have positive safety impacts, by allowing drivers to focus on the road rather than trying to figure out where to turn, alerting drivers to on-road cyclists, or pointing out potentially dangerous driving conditions (such as narrow roads).

Currently, signage directing visitors to MNWR is inadequate for drivers, cyclists, and even pedestrians. A lack of signage and the presence of signs with seemingly conflicting information (e.g. the distinction between public and private land) can cause drivers to unnecessarily slow down, use private drives as turn-arounds, and potentially prevent visitors from accessing the refuge.

MNWR has struggled to find the right balance between directional and informational signage for decades. As early as 1963, the MNWR manager outlined a signage plan suggesting a combination of different types of signs that would have made it easier for travelers to find and access the refuge.

Finally, improving traveler information would provide MNWR visitors with advanced information about parking, traffic conditions, and recreational opportunities. By providing more comprehensive information, MNWR could attract more visitors through outreach, and help visitors both access the refuge and fully understand all of the recreational and interpretive opportunities.

14.   Use variable message signs at new/redesigned intersection to direct visitors to satellite parking

Signage is a popular and effective way of managing traffic flow, particularly in congested areas. Traditional permanent signage can inform drivers and cyclists to merge, yield, or obey a certain speed limit. Signage that provides advance warning about congested areas, dangerous intersections, or other safety messages are also widely used by transportation planners.

However, Chatham's quaint village center and typical "New England" character are important local assets. Thus, in some cases there may be opposition to installing permanent directional signage throughout town. At the same time, some of the most serious congestion issues arise only during certain times of year (i.e. during particular summer weekends), making permanent signage unnecessary. An alternative to permanent posted signs is variable message signage.

Variable message signs (VMS) can take many different forms; permanent signs deliver traveler information and alerts, and are affixed to overpasses or large posts. In other cases, portable signs are used during roadway construction to deliver specific announcements to drivers (see photo below).

Permanent variable message sign   **Portable variable message sign**

Portable variable message signs can effectively re-route summer season traffic to satellite parking areas, or alert drivers to available shuttle service with access to Lighthouse Beach, MNWR, and other locations. In many cases, these portable signs include self-contained solar charging systems, obviating the need for an external power supply. Predefined messages can be stored in the unit, and a software package allows someone to administer the sign from a remote location. Costs for a trailer mounted VMS are approximately $18,000 to $19,000.

Portable VMSs can be trailer-mounted or pole mounted. For MNWR or the town of Chatham, a pole-mounted VMS would be easier to relocate to different areas of town. Available products typically display 1 to 3 lines of text or graphics and can include multi-screen messaging. These types of portable VMSs may cost slightly less than the larger trailer-mounted models.

A smaller alternative to a VMS is an arrow board. These pieces of equipment are smaller, and are only illuminated with an arrow pointing in a particular direction. They are not capable of being programmed to deliver different types of messages, and would be useful only in cases where it is essential to direct travelers to turn or merge. While limited in their ability to deliver complex information to drivers, they are much less costly than a VMS (average cost is $5,000).

Arrow board

Nearly all of the products that are available for purchase share similar design characteristics (in terms of color, materials, and size). This makes many of the VMSs potentially unappealing. One possibility for using a permanent VMS is to store the unit in a closed structure (e.g. a shed, lean-to, etc.) that mirrors the character of typical built structures in and around Chatham. Such a structure could offset the visual impact of the VMS while still delivering critical traveler information.

In terms of implementation, FWS may consider partnering with the town of Chatham or the Cape Cod Commission to share the costs of a portable sign and develop an agreement by which traffic information is delivered to refuge and beach visitors during the summer months. At other times of year, the town of Chatham may use the portable sign to deliver other types of messages. These signs are relatively low-cost, portable, programmable, and are able to be managed from remote locations (sometime with cell-phone based programming). Capital and operating costs could be shared by the town of Chatham, CCC, or MassDOT at the Queen Anne Road intersection project.

Some concerns include the visual impact of products that may be considered unsightly, limited value if used at only one intersection, and the challenge of agreeing upon priority locations. There are certainly maintenance burdens, for example storage when not in use, equitable use by partners (if shared asset), generating public support and identifying acceptable design with limited negative visual impact for residents and visitors.

15.   Improve bicycle route signage

One of Cape Cod's featured assets is the recently-expanded Cape Cod Rail Trail (CCRT). Formerly a working rail line, the ~22 mile rail trail stretches from South Dennis to Orleans, with a ~6 mile extension from Harwich to Chatham. Thousands of cyclists ride the trail each year; some access the Cape Cod National Seashore; others access the attractions in the many small village centers located adjacent to the trail.

The Chatham extension of the trail differs from the trail's "main line" in that it wends almost entirely through residential areas. There is virtually no commercial activity along the trail (e.g. bicycle shops, cafes, ice cream stores, etc.). The trail does not run contiguously from the Harwich CCRT bicycle rotary into downtown Chatham; multiple stretches of the trail run on local streets, and generally bypass Chatham's historic (but dense and sometimes congested) downtown.

In many cases it can be difficult for cyclists to be certain that they are riding on the designated bicycle route or the CCRT Chatham extension. Furthermore, available maps provide minimal information about proximity to recreational destinations or other assets. It is recommended that the on-street bicycle route be designated by new signage, to clarify the route. Such signage could also include directions to MNWR or Lighthouse Beach, etc. An example of such signage is pictured below. FWS could potentially help fund signs for the bicycle route and directions to MNWR, but the signs themselves would likely need to be installed by the town of Chatham, MassDOT, or the Massachusetts Department of Conservation and Recreation (which installed and maintains the CCRT).

Los Angeles' 4th Street Bikeway signage campaign.

One way to improve access to information about MNWR would be for FWS to work with the Town of Chatham and the Bikeways Committee to add information about MNWR to existing and planned bicycle information kiosks. Currently, there is only one formal bicycle information kiosk, located near the terminus of the Cape Cod Rail Trail Chatham Extension and the Chatham Elementary School. The kiosk provides information about Chatham destinations, bicycle-friendly routes throughout town, and locations of general amenities and services. There are large maps posted at the kiosk, and portable versions that cyclists can take with them. This effort is managed jointly by the Bikeways Committee and Town staff; both groups provide information and the Town prints the maps. While there is no available data on map usage, Town staff reported that the portable maps seem to be popular, and have not seen them littered on the ground around Chatham.

The initial kiosk is the first of its type, and there are plans to install two additional kiosks in spring 2010 at other bike path locations, potentially at George Ryder Road and Crowell Road. There is no formal plan for placing these new kiosks, which were formerly located at the Town Hall Annex. As funds become available to place the kiosks, the Town staff and the Bikeways Committee will consider the next appropriate locations.

The information and maps provided at the kiosk do not currently reference MNWR or South Beach. The Town staff indicated that references to MNWR and South Beach could be easily added to the kiosks and maps, in order to promote these public destinations. FWS may also find opportunities to provide support for the kiosks and maps, by contributing funds for map production or for obtaining and installing additional kiosks.

16.   Improve directional signage to MNWR Headquarters/Visitor Contact Station

Should FWS move forward with acquisition or construction of a visitor contact station in downtown Chatham, directional signage for vehicular, bicycle, and pedestrian traffic will be critical. Signage plans developed in the 1960s and later provide useful guidance on signage locations.

There are a variety of options for incorporating directional signage to the visitor contact station in Chatham. Specific areas of confusion are clustered around the intersection of Main Street and Shore Road, at the Morris Island Road fork with Little Beach Road, and at the head of Tisquantum Road.

Discrete directional signs can be erected to divert motorists, cyclists, and pedestrians away from private neighborhoods and toward the refuge. Additionally, portable signage such as freestanding pavements signs (see photo) can be obtained for as little as $300 per sign. For particularly high-visitation weekends, signs like these can eliminate traveler confusion without becoming permanent fixtures in the neighborhood.

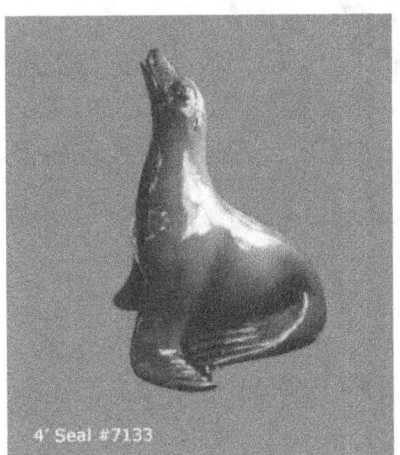

This large fiberglass seal can be part of a playful campaign to direct visitors to MNWR.

Another option for creating and installing directional signage to the MNWR headquarters/visitor contact station incorporates elements of a public art and education campaign. MNWR could conceive of educational displays about Monomoy's wildlife that are strategically located at intersections where directional signage to the headquarters/visitor contact station is absent or insufficient. These signs could offer limited environmental information or highlight a particular piece of flora/fauna at Monomoy (such as a tern) paired with clear and discrete directional information.

Costs for these kinds of projects can vary greatly depending on scope. Larger public art installations (such as the seal above) may cost between $1,000 and $5,000 per item. Planning and design services could be donated by landscape architecture students, or contracted out at hourly rates, with complete signage planning projects costing between $10,000 and $50,000 depending on the scope of the effort.

17.   Add directional and informational signage throughout the Town of Chatham

Local signage can be used to better direct travelers to the headquarters/visitor contact station from downtown Chatham. There are very few signs that identify MNWR and no signage in historic downtown Chatham (Main Street) that suggests a preferred route to the headquarters/visitor contact station.

Signs can be large or small (see photos below); signage recommended years ago by FWS staff included directional signs approximately 1.5' x 2.5' and several larger informational signs approximately 3-4 feet tall and 4-6 feet wide.

Historical signage costs appear to be in line with today's costs: median price for municipal signs is approximately $100, though the range is large ($25 to $150); FWS narratives refer to a total cost of $550 for six signs of various sizes.

18.   Add directional and information signage throughout Cape Cod and along Route 6

MNWR narratives indicate that FWS staff has identified potential sign locations around Cape Cod at different points in MNWR's history. Such signs would point to MNWR from various locations, including off Route 6, the Hyannis Rotary, and the Orleans Rotary.

Additional signage (whether limited to directional arrows or expanded narrative information) can establish a more visible presence for MNWR in the larger Cape region. Signage can be used to promote existing or new headquarters/visitor contact station amenities (e.g., exhibits, bicycle and pedestrian facilities, Island tours). Signage costs could be shared with CACO or DCR by erecting signs that promote multiple public sites and attractions (such as the CCRT, MNWR, or CACO Visitor Center), especially if the existing right of way is used.

There are some considerations and challenges associated with a regional signage campaign. For example, complementary appropriate local signage or directions would be necessary at Route 6 locations, bridges, or outlying locations. Finally, signage maintenance (repainting, structural maintenance) would need to be agreed upon with stakeholders, possibly through a Memorandum of Understanding or a Memorandum of Agreement.

19.   Improve traveler information on MNWR website

While the MNWR website provides visitors with a wealth of information about the history and conservation performed at the refuge, it provides little information about how to access the refuge. Directions and closed areas are listed, but there are no details regarding traveler information and parking. By improving the website, MNWR could provide general information about travel to and visiting the refuge, as well as detailed information that could be updated as conditions change. Such ability will be particularly important if MNWR decides to undertake other actions such as parking restrictions, satellite parking and shuttle service, etc.

An overhaul of the existing website to improve readability and navigation would cost between $5,000 and $15,000. This would include making travel information more obvious, and adding missing pieces of travel information. This would also include organization of existing documents and ensuring Section 508 compliance. Any overhaul would need to be made in concert with a planned implementation of a consistent FWS website template.

MNWR could also utilize the website technology to provide visitors with up to date travel information. For example, MNWR could indicate to travelers if the parking lot is full or if the causeway is congested. This would require staff with technical abilities to regularly update the website.

Other Interventions

Some interventions do not fall neatly into a single category. These ideas are forward-thinking, innovative, and are not necessarily exclusively focused on transportation. For example, creating an MNWR visitor contact station in or near downtown Chatham would provide the refuge with increased visibility and additional office space. Due to the location of the current MNWR Headquarters, the refuge encounters fewer unplanned visits than more central attractions. If a visitor contact station were located in or near downtown Chatham, tourists might stop and inquire about the refuge, learning more about its recreational and educational opportunities. Furthermore, a larger building than the current MNWR Headquarters, would allow space for concessionaires and greater educational and interpretive resources.

20.   Relocate MNWR Visitor Contact Station

Relocating the NMWR visitor contact station from its current location on Morris Island, to somewhere within Downtown Chatham would significantly improve the visibility of the refuge, and allow MNWR to make meaningful and measurable transportation improvements. The study team's analysis of the feasibility of relocating the visitor contact station or constructing a new visitor contact station focuses almost exclusively on the transportation-related requirements and considerations. There are many other strategic, economic, and ecological considerations that are not addressed here, and should be discussed by FWS staff and stakeholders.

There are three primary potential areas for a new MNWR visitor contact station: on Main Street (Rte 28) just west of the densest area of Downtown Chatham, on Old Harbor Road (Rte 28), or along Oyster Pond, the start of the Oyster River. Relocation of the visitor contact station is most limited by the availability of space in the targeted areas. The three areas are shown in Map 12.

All three locations would allow the visitor contact station to provide pedestrian, bicycle, automobile, and shuttle access; however, only the Oyster Pond/Oyster River site would also allow waterfront access. With a new central visitor contact station, concessionaires that tour the Monomoy Islands, as well as tour the Morris Island portion of the refuge could pick up visitors at and depart directly from the new visitor contact station.

Presently there are properties available in all three of the targeted areas, however once the funds are dedicated to the visitor contact station project, MNWR may need to wait until an appropriate property becomes available, purchase a property in a slightly less desired location or work with the town of Chatham to acquire a town-owned property. Alternatively, MNWR could lease a site Downtown, until a property becomes available for purchase.

Map 12: Potential Alternate Visitor Contact Station Locations

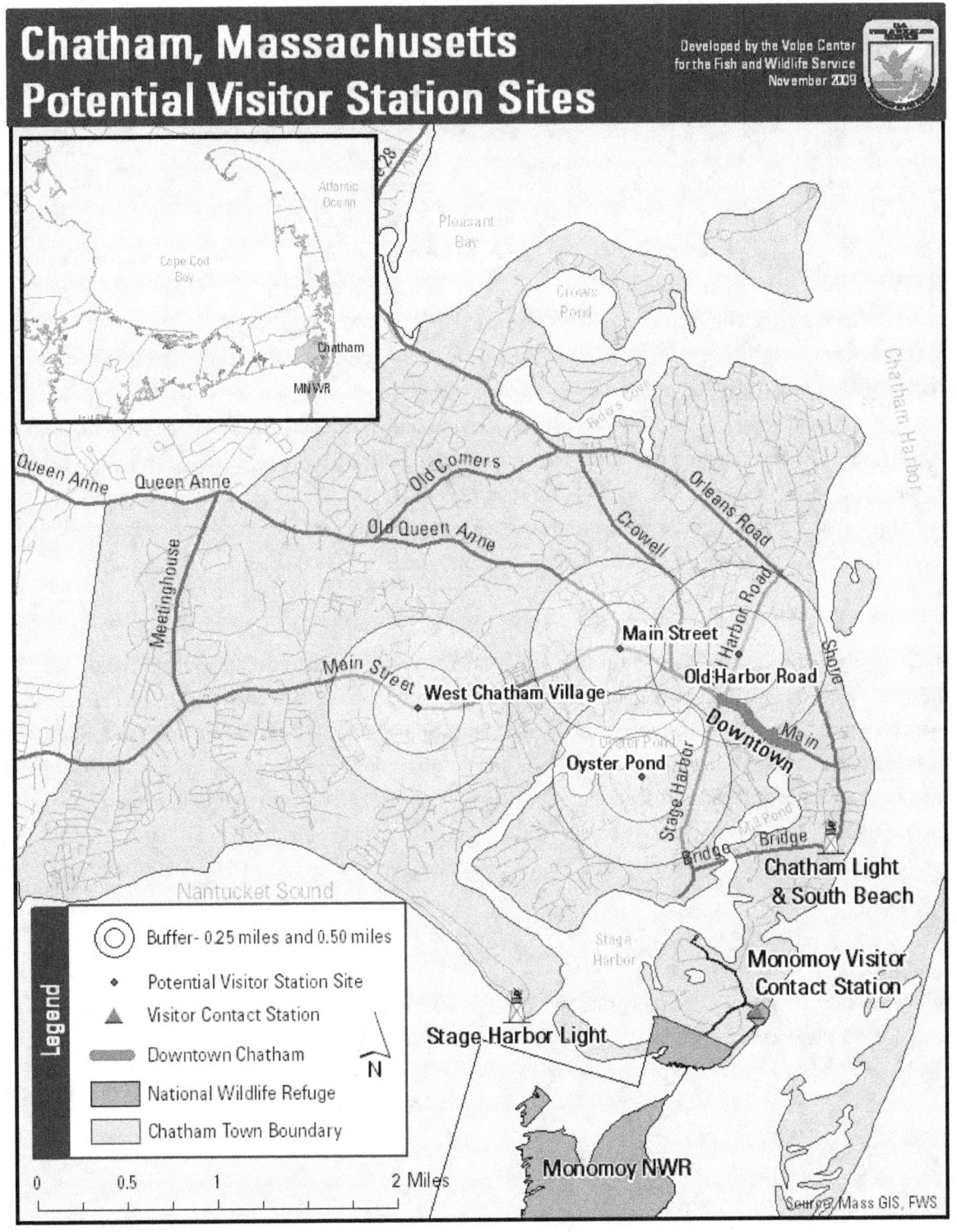

Space Requirements

Commercial property in Chatham, for ownership, costs on average $382.62 per square foot of "living space" (based on a small sample of commercial spaces downtown). Existing interior spaces range in size from 1,000–5,000 square feet. In this range, MNWR should be able to locate an adequate property to house the visitor contact station, administrative services, and depending on the location, staff lodging. If MNWR obtained building permits, it would be able to either demolish and create a new building, or build on a vacant lot.

In order to accommodate all of the intended modes of transportation, and a new MNWR visitor contact station, a land parcel would be at least 20,000 square feet, with 3,000-5,000 square feet of either existing or buildable space for the visitor contact station building. The indoor space could contain administrative offices, visitor services, interpretive exhibits and visitor information. If additional space were acquired, the visitor contact station could share its site with housing for MNWR staff.

Parking at the Visitor Contact Station

In order to accommodate a range of visitor types, and provide added benefit to the town of Chatham, the parking lot at the visitor contact station would have a capacity of at least 100 cars. A typical parking space is 8-10 feet wide and 18-20 feet deep, totaling 144-200 square feet. Off-street parking typically requires 300-350 square feet per space, including access lanes and landscaping, allowing 100-150 spaces per acre, depending on design. Surface parking lot construction costs average approximately $5,000 per space, not including the cost of the land. [32]

When designing the parking lot it will be critical to consider the paving material. Due to the location and hydrology of Chatham, it would be both environmentally sensitive and cost effective to select a permeable or pervious paving surface. Using such a material would significantly control stormwater run-off. Pervious materials include poured pervious surfaces, pervious concrete, pervious pavers or sand/crushed shells. Pervious surfaces other than sand/crushed shells, cost anywhere from 50 cents to four dollars more per square foot for installation; however, these values do not reflect the cost savings of using the pervious surface in stormwater management and long-term care (if traditional pavement is used, then additional stormwater management may be required).

Potential Sites

The following sites are sampling of properties that are available in each of the three target areas. Each area has different strengths and weaknesses.

---

[32] Transportation Cost and Benefit Analysis II – Parking Costs, Victoria Transport Policy Institute. http://www.vtpi.org/tca/tca0504.pdf

Downtown Chatham

1010 Main St, Chatham, MA 02669

Price: $589,900

Lot Size: 21,780 square feet

Living Area: 2,247 square feet

Source: Multiple Listing Service (MLS)

This property located just outside of Downtown Chatham provides the opportunity to be on Chatham's main roadway. In addition to proximity to Downtown, the property is located one half to one mile from the beach, and zoned for a small business.

The sidewalks and crosswalks along Main Street offer safe pedestrian access, and the well-marked roads are usable for bicyclists. At the same time, the road is wide enough, with primarily commercial properties, and would easily support transit, or a satellite parking location.

The primary drawback of this location is that is not directly in the Downtown area; however, with the addition of a shuttle that stops near the downtown, this could easily be a viable location.

Old Harbor Road (Rte 28)

151 Old Harbor Rd, Chatham, MA 02633

Price: $1,150,000

Lot Size: 30,056 square feet

Living Area: 2,677 square feet

Source: Multiple Listing Service (MLS)

This property is in the downtown area at the intersection of Old Harbor Road (Rte. 28) and Old Academy. The buildings on the property presently include a large farmhouse and barn, which could be repurposed or demolished. The property exceeds the size requirement for the visitor contact station. Nearby parking lots suggest a precedent that putting a parking lot on this property would be appropriate and feasible.

This location supports multiple modes of transportation. It is less than a mile from many attractions in Downtown Chatham, making it an ideal location for pedestrians walking to and from town, bicyclists visiting the local area, and satellite parking for the Downtown area. Its placement on a major roadway makes it easily identifiable, and accessible for small transit vehicles.

There are few drawbacks to locating the visitor contact station along Old Harbor Road (Rte. 28) as it is well located and a major thoroughfare.

Oyster Pond

63 Oyster Bay Lane, Chatham, MA 02633
Price: $1,599,000
Lot Size: 45,738 square feet
Living Area: 2,592 square feet

Source: Multiple Listing Service (MLS)

This large property is located approximately one mile from Downtown Chatham, and boasts both deeded beach rights on Oyster Pond and deep water access. These features would make this location ideal for waterfront activities at the visitor contact station, and access to MNWR via the Oyster River.

This property, and most along Oyster Pond, poses major drawbacks; with the exception of a few properties held by the town, or a conservation organization, most properties are located at the end of long and narrow residential streets. While this might be accessible to bicyclists and pedestrians, it would be difficult for transit vehicles to travel down these streets, and unpalatable to neighbors to have a large number of automobiles traveling down these roads.

West Chatham Village

Another potential alternate location for the visitor contact station is in West Chatham Village, located at the intersection of George Ryder Road, Route 28 and Barn Hill Road. This site is roughly 3-4 miles from Morris Island. The area is a priority redevelopment district for the Town of Chatham, with plans to create an alternate commercial center, possibly anchored by a municipal or government office. Such a revitalization project presents an opportunity for MNWR to acquire a space in a neighborhood that would cost less than in Chatham's historic downtown, but may -- in the near future – have similar visibility and destination appeal. This space would have ample parking, and could still have many of the same amenities as a downtown site.

Rental Space

Renting a storefront in downtown Chatham would provide MNWR with a presence in downtown Chatham. Rental spaces tend to be less than 1000 square feet and do not have on site parking. Rental rates are steep, but not cost prohibitive; storefront space generally rents between $30.00 and $60.00 per square foot, per year.

While rental storefront space might not allow MNWR to provide alternate parking for visitors, or to move all operations to the downtown area, a downtown space could host many interpretive exhibits and serve as a base for concessionaires, such as the Monomoy ferries, and as an information station about the visitor opportunities at the refuge. Having a rental visitor contact station would also allow MNWR to give directional information to visitors that might otherwise have difficulty finding the refuge on Morris Island.

Renting a downtown space before purchasing a space would allow MNWR to determine the feasibility and value of having a location downtown.

21. Improve waterfront access (for ferries to the Monomoy Islands)

Presently there are two forms of waterfront access to MNWR. The first is through concessionaires, such as the Outermost or Rip Ryder ferry services. The second is through the on-site MNWR water access point.

Both current waterfront access methods present some drawbacks – in order to reach the Monomoy Islands, visitors must either go to a private dock, or utilize the non-handicapped accessible MNWR access point (visitors must enter the water to get aboard the boat). Both accessibility and visitor experience could be improved by adding an additional point of waterfront access.

Acquiring additional dock space or a waterfront site would allow MNWR staff and visitors to access all parts of the refuge, including the Monomoy Islands and Morris Island, from one central location. Due to the sand drifts, the most viable waterfront spaces would be Stage Harbor, Mill Pond, Oyster Pond and Oyster River. Space in either Stage Harbor or Oyster Pond would be the most preferred options as Stage Harbor is near the refuge and Oyster Pond is near Downtown Chatham.

In order to acquire additional waterfront access, MNWR would either need to obtain a town mooring, or purchase a waterfront parcel of land. Both options present opportunities and limitations.

1. Town Mooring

In order to obtain a town mooring, MNWR would need to request a spot on the wait list for its desired mooring site. The wait period for a town mooring at any of the preferred locations is approximately 10-20 years. While this option may take years before it is operational, there would be minimal environmental permitting issues, as the space is already used for mooring purposes.

If MNWR obtained a town mooring, the mooring would be subject to all regulations as well as mooring fees. The mooring fee structure is as follows:

(a) Private moorings, resident or non-resident taxpayer	
All vessels, length overall	$2.50 / foot
"Mooring Only"	$40.00
(b) Private moorings for non-residents:	
All vessels, length overall	$6.00 / foot
"Mooring Only"	$80.00
(c) Renters of commercial rental moorings / slips	
Resident or Non-resident taxpayer: All vessels, length overall	$2.50 / foot
Non-resident: All vessels, length overall	$6.00 / foot
(d) Commercial / Rental Moorings (Marina / Boatyard):	
For each mooring available for rent to the General public	$150.00
(e) Town Transient Moorings	
Resident or Non-resident taxpayer	N/C
Non-resident - Current mooring permit holder	$10.00 per night
Non resident - Transient	$25.00 per night
(f) Waiting list fees	
Resident / Non-resident taxpayer: Initial fee / Annual renewal fee	$5.00 / boat
Non-resident: Initial fee / Annual renewal fee	$15.00 / boat

Source: Town of Chatham

MNWR would need to establish the mooring fee as an annual budget item, if this option were selected.

2. Purchase a Waterfront Site

Purchasing a waterfront site, though expensive at the onset, would allow MNWR the option to build docks, moorings, related buildings, parking, or transit, bicycle and pedestrian facilities. The two target locations, Oyster Pond and Stage Harbor, are both easily accessible by road and water. Properties on Stage Harbor are generally residential; however, both existing buildings and "buildable" waterfront lots are available. The proximity of this location to the refuge itself is its primary advantage; however, in order to access this location, visitors will still need to travel from Downtown Chatham. While properties in this area might exclude general pedestrian traffic, it would still allow for bicycle, automobile and transit access, especially if the property were located on Bridge Street or Stage Island Road.

Properties on Oyster Pond have both residential and municipal functions. This location is accessible to Downtown Chatham although lot sizes tend to be smaller than on Stage Harbor. If MNWR acquired a location on Oyster Pond, it could serve as both a visitor contact station and as a waterfront access point.

6. ALTERNATIVE TRANSPORTATION SCENARIOS

The study team developed four scenarios for implementing alternative transportation improvements. The scenarios are comprised of several interventions designed to produce certain outcomes and have particular impacts on the way the transportation system functions in the MNWR and Chatham areas. Each scenario seeks to address problems identified during the Monomoy Transportation Assistance Group (TAG) meeting, held in July 2007. The scenarios also seek to address or ameliorate issues identified during the existing conditions research phase, and are responsive to the ideas suggested by stakeholders (both the general public and local entities). Table 13 shows the list of interventions and which ones are present in each scenario.

6.1. Developing the Scenarios

The four scenarios were developed by combining several interventions, to meet multiple project goals. The scenarios are intended to provide various examples of how alternative transportation access improvements could be approached, with some scenarios requiring more technically complicated interventions than others. A scenario might highlight a particular mode of transportation, such as transit, or it may highlight particular strategies or approaches, like leveraging local and regional partnerships or implementing Intelligent Transportation Systems (ITS) solutions. The scenarios represent a range of cost and implementation complexity options, in order to provide multiple possibilities for FWS to consider in planning for the future.

It is important to note that the scenarios are not mutually exclusive – it might be possible to implement one scenario as a short-term measure, while preparing to implement another scenario once funding or other needs are met. In addition, it is important to recognize that each scenario is comprised of several interventions, some of which must be combined in order for the scenario to achieve its expected outcome. In other cases, FWS could choose to implement one or more of the interventions included in a scenario, but not all.

The "description" section of each write-up provides an overview of each scenario's elements. The "discussion" section for each scenario provides a rationale for linking interventions in order to achieve project goals and answers questions such as "how do these interventions work together?", "what is the feasibility of implementing this scenario?", and "what are the strengths/weaknesses, opportunities, and hurdles associated with this scenario?".

Table 13: Scenario-Intervention Matrix

ELEMENT		Scenario 1 Satellite parking and transit service	Scenario 2 Relocated MNWR visitor contact station	Scenario 3 Roadway safety improvements	Scenario 4 Nonmotorized transportation improvements
1	Relocate and reinstall Causeway fencing to better accommodate parked cars and emergency vehicles			X	
2	Create multi-use path on one side of Causeway for bicycles and pedestrians				X
3	Construct sidewalk between Bridge Street parking areas and Lighthouse Beach			X	
4	Paint "Sharrow" or shared lane markings on signed bicycle route for bicycles				X
5	Provide bicycle facilities/amenities with shuttle service	X			
6	Provide pedestrian improvements at and around shuttle stops	X			
7	Add bicycle and pedestrian facilities and amenities at new visitor contact station		X		
8	Provide additional bicycle racks at visitor contact station, Lighthouse Beach, and high priority downtown locations				X
9	Identify/secure a satellite parking location	X			
10	Implement parking restrictions at visitor contact station	X			
11	Operate shuttle service to MNWR and throughout Chatham from satellite parking	X			
12	Contract with taxi service or other provider to offer demand responsive, shared taxi service to MNWR	X			

6. Alternative Transportation Scenarios — Monomoy National Wildlife Refuge Alternative Transportation Study

		Scenario 1	Scenario 2	Scenario 3	Scenario 4
	(and other destinations in Chatham) from satellite parking				
13	Provide a multi-passenger shuttle from a new Downtown Visitor Center to Morris Island		X		
14	Use variable message signs at new/redesigned intersection to direct visitors to satellite parking	X			
15	Improve bicycle route signage	X		X	X
16	Improve directional signage to MNWR visitor contact station		X		X
17	Add directional and informational signage throughout the town of Chatham	X	X	X	X
18	Add directional and information signage throughout Cape Cod and along Route 6	X	X	X	X
19	Improve traveler information on MNWR website	X	X	X	X
20	Relocate MNWR visitor contact station		X		
21	Improve waterfront access (for ferries to the Monomoy Islands)				

6.2. Evaluating the Scenarios

The project team developed evaluation criteria for each scenario, based on the project goals described in Chapter 1. The criteria fall into the following five broad areas:

- Access
- Traffic and Parking
- Safety
- Visitor Experience
- Feasibility

For each scenario, the project team considered whether the suite of interventions was **likely** to achieve the goal, could **possibly** achieve the goal, was **unlikely** to achieve the goal, or was **not applicable**. The assessments are qualitative, and meant to describe the potential implications of implementing a given scenario. The feasibility determinations are based on combining the relevant ratings of the group of interventions included in a particular scenario. The ratings and assessment are intended to evaluate the ability of each scenario to address particular project goals, as well as potential unintended consequences of the scenarios (e.g., improved traveler information generating more private vehicle access and increased traffic congestion). The descriptions and analyses of each scenario address the implementation considerations.

The evaluation matrix for the four scenarios is provided in Table 14. More detailed cost estimates for each scenario are provided in APPENDIX F.

6. Alternative Transportation Scenarios | Monomoy National Wildlife Refuge Alternative Transportation Study

Table 14: Scenario Evaluation Matrix

Criteria	Scenario 1	Scenario 2	Scenario 3	Scenario 4
Access				
Improves pedestrian/bicycle access to MNWR	?	✓	?	✓
Provides transit service to MNWR	✓	?	N/A	N/A
Provides alternate water access options to Monomoy Islands	N/A	✓	N/A	N/A
Provides connections to existing regional transit service	✓	?	?	?
Traffic & Parking				
Facilitates reduction in traffic congestion in downtown Chatham	✓	?	-	?
Facilitates reduction in traffic congestion around Morris Island	✓	✓	?	✓
Reduces parking pressure at Morris Island	✓	✓	?	✓
Safety				
Improves traveler safety on Causeway	?	✓	✓	✓
Improves traveler safety on Bridge St.	?	?	✓	?
Improves visitor wayfinding	✓	✓	✓	✓
Improves visitor awareness/knowledge about MNWR	✓	✓	✓	✓
Feasibility				
Expected cost range	High	Very High	Low-Med	Low
Technical difficulty of implementation	Med	Med	Med	Med
Implementation time frame	2-5 years	5+ years	1-2 years	2-5 years
Potential political sensitivity of implementation	Med-High	Med	Low-Med	Low
Potential for public approval / support for implementation	Med-High	High	Med-High	High

Key

✓ Likely

- Unlikely

? Possibly

N/A Not applicable

6.3.   Scenario 1: Alleviate Traffic Congestion and Parking Limitations with Satellite Parking and Shuttle Service

This scenario seeks to alleviate traffic congestion and to expand limited parking options for visitors to MNWR and other popular destinations. Strategic outcomes and expected impacts include:

- Relieve vehicular traffic congestion in downtown Chatham and in the Quitnesset area approach to MNWR;
- Alleviate capacity issues at existing parking lots and areas;
- Expand alternative transportation options, namely transit service, to MNWR and other similar visitor destinations; and
- Reduce or eliminate confusion/unawareness of travel options for MNWR and Chatham area visitors.

Transportation is an interconnected system or network. Changes to one aspect of the network can have far-reaching impacts on other parts of the network or on entirely different networks (i.e. the connection between transportation and housing development). In this scenario, immediate or "first-level" anticipated impacts include congestion relief and use of transit service. Later ("second-level" or "third-level") impacts can include improved safety and crash reduction (by reducing the number of vehicles in a congested area) and increased visitation to MNWR (by promoting travel options and providing parking and shuttle service).

> **SCENARIO 1 INTERVENTIONS:**
>
> Identify and secure a satellite parking location
>
> Operate shuttle service to MNWR and other destinations
>
> Improve signage and wayfinding
>
> Implement Visitor Center parking restrictions
>
> Install pedestrian improvements at Main St./Queen Anne Rd. rotary and shuttle stops
>
> Provide bicycle facilities and amenities at shuttle stops
>
> Use variable message signs at new/redesigned intersection to direct visitors to satellite parking
>
> Improve traveler information on the MNWR Web site

Description

The sidebar at right provides the list of interventions included in Scenario 1. More information is provided in Table 15. A satellite parking lot, most likely at the Chatham Junior/Senior High School or Elementary School, coupled with seasonal shuttle service to MNWR and other destinations within Chatham is the backbone of this scenario. Given the current limitations to expanding the regional transit system within Chatham, the shuttle service envisioned in this scenario would operate only within Chatham and likely by an independent operator (rather than by the CCRTA). Connections to existing regional H2O service can be arranged through strategic transfer points and shuttle stops.

Companion interventions include the establishment of parking restrictions at MNWR Headquarters to provide an incentive or requirement that visitors wishing to access the site would not be able to do so via personal automobiles. Provision of pedestrian and bicycle amenities at and around the shuttle stops and bicycle racks on the vehicles would help to provide multi-modal access to the shuttle, so that visitors could choose to access via satellite parking or foot or bicycle.

Finally, Scenario 1 also includes an enhanced traveler information campaign to assist visitors in accessing MNWR by shuttle, bicycle, foot, or car. An information and outreach campaign could feature printed or Web-based information specific to the alternate parking and shuttle service, as well as general signage and information regarding the refuge. For example, technology such as portable variable messaging signs could alert travelers to the shuttle service and direct them to the satellite parking location. Such signs could be incorporated into the redesigned intersection of Main Street, Queen Anne Road, Crowell Road, and Depot Road, or at other appropriate locations. Additionally, directions on the MNWR Web site could include information about the shuttle, as well as information on how to reach the refuge by bicycle, and preferred routes based on mode of transportation. Overall improved signage in Chatham and around Morris Island could reduce visitor confusion and facilitate multi-modal access throughout Chatham and to the refuge.

Discussion

This scenario is designed to meet the project goals of providing transit services to MNWR, with connections to the regional transit system. A local shuttle option serving downtown, Lighthouse Beach, and MNWR is expected to reduce some traffic and parking pressure in all of these areas, particularly if travelers are well-informed about its availability and have incentives to use it (or limitations on travel and parking in these areas). These interventions – traveler information, satellite parking, and shuttle service are most effective when implemented in tandem. For example, given the distance of the schools from MNWR (over two miles), it would be essential to provide some sort of shuttle or demand-response taxi service to bring visitors to the refuge, Lighthouse Beach, or downtown. Note that a shuttle could potentially operate *without* a satellite parking facility; shuttles could pick up and drop off passengers at agreed-upon locations. However, this option would likely have little to no impact on congestion (since there would not be a new place to store vehicles other than the existing lots and roadways).

It must be noted that no survey of traveler demand for transit to/from Monomoy has been conducted. There is no existing data on the anticipated number of drivers who could be channeled to a satellite parking facility, nor is there specific information about the anticipated number of riders who would make use of a free or paid shuttle bus or demand response taxi.

While this scenario does not include physical changes to Bridge Street or the Causeway, it may impact traveler safety on these facilities. It could improve traveler safety on the Causeway by reducing the number of cars driving to or parking on the Causeway when trying to access MNWR. Alternatively, it could exacerbate issues on the Causeway either by encouraging more people to park there (as a result of parking limitations at MNWR Headquarters), or by introducing the shuttle vehicle among existing Causeway use. Similarly, it could improve traveler safety on Bridge Street by reducing the number of cars driving to or parking on Bridge Street trying to access Lighthouse Beach. However, introduction of a shuttle vehicle among existing traffic and parking could also exacerbate existing conflicts.

While this scenario does not provide specific pedestrian or bicycle infrastructure, improved bicycle route signage could promote overall bicycle travel in Chatham and facilitate access to MNWR. Improved transit connections, both locally and regionally, could also allow access by foot or bicycle to the shuttle service.

Depending on the scale of shuttle service provided, full implementation of Scenario 1 could exceed $400-500,000. Some of this cost would be one-time capital costs, such as acquisition of shuttle vehicles, with additional needs for ongoing shuttle operations and maintenance. Developing a service plan and securing funding and vehicles could take up to five or more years. Narrow roadways and the neighborhood character along the shuttle route would likely dictate a relatively small shuttle vehicle, which could alleviate some public concerns about noise and other impacts on the downtown or adjacent neighborhoods. If these concerns can be addressed, then this scenario could have high public approval, as it would provide a useful and needed service, while reducing traffic congestion and visitor confusion.

Table 15: Summary Scenario 1 – Satellite Parking and Shuttle Service

SCENARIO 1 ELEMENT	COST	IMPLEMENTATION TIME FRAME	PARTNERSHIPS
Satellite parking	Minimal – would be arranged through agreement	MEDIUM: Within 1-2 years PHASES: • Partner agreement • Site planning / engineering / signage • Implementation and management • Marketing and promotion	Town of Chatham, School Department
Use variable message signs at new/redesigned intersection to direct visitors to satellite parking	$5,000 to $20,000 per sign	SHORT: within 1 year PHASES: • Site planning and purchase • Implementation and maintenance	Town of Chatham, Cape Cod Commission, Mass Department of Transportation
Shuttle Service	$195,000 per season for operations and maintenance of two vehicles $15,000 to $150,000 per vehicle	LONG: Within 5 years or longer PHASES: • Funding • Transit planning • Vehicle purchase • Operations and maintenance • Marketing and promotion	Town of Chatham, Cape Cod Commission, Cape Cod Regional Transit Authority, independent bus companies, other operator

6. Alternative Transportation Scenarios   Monomoy National Wildlife Refuge Alternative Transportation Study

SCENARIO 1

ELEMENT	COST	IMPLEMENTATION TIME FRAME	PARTNERSHIPS
Provide bicycle facilities/amenities at shuttle stops	$100 to $700 per bike rack (depending on design and number of bikes. Does not include installation) $10,000 to $15,000 per bus shelter (depending on size and design) $100 to $500 per trash receptacle (more for solar compacting receptacles) Outdoor bulletin boards with traveler information as low as $200; electronic kiosks range from $1,000 to $8,000	MEDIUM: Within 1-2 years PHASES: • Funding • Planning and design • Installation	Town of Chatham, Cape Cod Regional Transit Authority, Cape Cod Commission; Chatham Chamber of Commerce; Chatham Downtown Business Association
Add directional and informational signage throughout Chatham	~$100 for directional or informational signs; several thousand dollars for coordinated wayfinding campaign.	MEDIUM: Within 1-2 years PHASES: • Funding • Planning and design • Installation	Town of Chatham, Mass Department of Transportation
Add directional and information signage throughout Cape Cod and along Route 6	~$100 for directional or informational signs; several thousand dollars for coordinated wayfinding campaign.	LONG: Within 5 years PHASES: • Agreement with multiple jurisdictions about signage placement • Funding • Planning and design • Installation	Cape Cod Commission, Mass Department of Transportation, Mass Department of Conservation and Recreation, other towns
Improve bicycle route signage	~$100 per sign	MEDIUM: Within 1-2 years PHASES: • Funding	Town of Chatham, Bicycle Commission, Mass Department of Transportation

6. Alternative Transportation Scenarios   Monomoy National Wildlife Refuge Alternative Transportation Study

SCENARIO 1 ELEMENT	COST	IMPLEMENTATION TIME FRAME	PARTNERSHIPS
Parking restrictions at headquarters/visitor contact station	$0 - $20,000 – excluding staff resources	SHORT: within 1 year PHASES: • Planning and design • Installation • Planning • Implementation	Coordination with Friends groups, ferry operators, provide information to general public
Pedestrian improvements at and around shuttle stops	~$2-4,000 each for user activated pedestrian signals ~$60-80/ft for sidewalk construction	MEDIUM - LONG: 1 to 5 years PHASES: • Agreement with Town/MHD about improvements • Funding • Planning and design • Purchase and installation • Maintenance	Town of Chatham, Mass Department of Transportation
Improve traveler information on MNWR website	$0 - $20,000 depending on scope of changes	SHORT: within 1 year PHASES: • Plan content updates and site improvements • Publish updates	None – internal

6.4. Scenario 2: Relocation of Monomoy Visitor Contact Station

This scenario addresses specific transportation issues, such as congestion, parking limitations, and traveler confusion by recommending establishment of a visitor contact station closer to downtown Chatham, either in addition to or in place of the current facility on Morris Island. Strategic outcomes and expected impacts include:

- Improved vehicular access to the headquarters/ visitor contact station;
- Improved bicycle and pedestrian access to the headquarters/ visitor contact station; and
- Reduced confusion or lack of knowledge among Cape visitors regarding MNWR as a recreational asset, and travel options to reach MNWR.

In this scenario, immediate or "first-level" anticipated impacts include improved access to the headquarters/ visitor contact station ("second-level" or "third-level") impacts can include reduced traffic congestion on the Morris Island Road causeway or in the neighborhoods on Morris Island (if a visitor contact station is relocated), increased access via nonmotorized travel modes, and increased visitation to MNWR (by relocating to a more visible and accessible location in Chatham, and better promoting travel options).

> **SCENARIO 2 INTERVENTIONS:**
>
> Relocate MNWR visitor contact station (including all administrative activities, exhibits, and other services) to downtown Chatham
>
> Add bicycle and pedestrian facilities and amenities at new visitor contact station
>
> Provide a shuttle to the ferry from new downtown visitor contact station
>
> Identify alternate dock space for Monomoy ferries
>
> Improve directional signage to MNWR headquarters/visitor contact station
>
> Add directional and informational signage throughout Chatham
>
> Add directional and information signage throughout Cape Cod and along Route 6

Description

The sidebar at right provides the list of interventions suggested for inclusion in Scenario 2. More information is provided in Table 16. An alternate space for the MNWR Headquarters could be obtained by either: (1) relocating the existing visitor contact station to a downtown or other location off of Morris Island, or (2) constructing a larger visitor contact station in accordance with FWS guidelines for Refuge Visitor Centers. The scenario is successfully implemented by pairing major capital investments (e.g. construction or relocation) with smaller capital investments in signage and outreach/communications campaigns to improve traveler information.

It should be noted that if capital investments are not feasible at this time, it is still possible to achieve the strategic goals listed above *to a limited degree*. Printed or Web-based directional and informational materials are valuable on their own, but would have smaller transportation impacts than major capital improvements such as relocation.

Discussion

This scenario is designed to meet the project goals of reducing traffic and parking congestion around MNWR and within Chatham, enhancing the visitor experience, and developing and enhancing partnerships with governmental and non-governmental agencies.

The first element of the scenario involves establishing a visitor contact station near downtown Chatham or another location off of Morris Island, accessible by foot from downtown Chatham or other key Chatham destinations. Transportation amenities or facilities could include an expanded parking area for vehicular travelers, and more bicycle parking than is available at the current Morris Island location. The relocated visitor contact station could potentially be housed in a shared space with another entity (such as the Chatham Chamber of Commerce, the MA Department of Conservation and Recreation, or another group with a similar public purpose or mission). As a companion to such a move, FWS would need to partner with the Town of Chatham or other stakeholder to engage in a coordinated and targeted marketing campaign to encourage visitation to the visitor contact station. In order to address the transportation needs of most visitors, this scenario would require that FWS or its partners offer a shuttle service from a downtown or other location to the ferries that bring visitors to the Islands. A 15-passenger van was used as an example shuttle vehicle in order to provide a cost estimate.

The second element of the scenario features constructing a larger visitor contact station off of Morris Island. Again, a shuttle would need to be provided for visitors going to the ferries. From a transportation perspective, a benefit of constructing a larger visitor contact station would allow FWS to combine transportation services and facilities in a single location. The site could include ample surface parking, but also feature secure bicycle parking and amenities (described in "Interventions"), pedestrian amenities (e.g. benches, maps, etc.), and transit or shuttle stops. The visitor contact station could serve as a transportation hub not only for MNWR but for other nearby attractions in Chatham.

Implementation of Scenario 2 could lead to reduced traffic congestion in downtown Chatham and around Morris Island, as it would reduce the number of vehicles traveling to the current headquarters/ visitor contact station for short visits. There would be fewer MNWR visitors traveling to Morris Island, and those that did, would be more likely to stay for longer periods of time than those who currently come for a brief visit and then drive back through downtown Chatham. It would also enhance the visitor experience by providing clearer opportunities for obtaining information about and visiting MNWR. While the scenario does not include physical changes to any roadways, some level of increased roadway safety would be anticipated if there is significant reduction in traffic. Depending on the location of the new site, it would likely foster more opportunities for access to the visitor contact station through alternate modes of transportation.

It would be possible for FWS to phase implementation of Scenario 2. If directional and information signage campaigns are undertaken, FWS may wish to start by improving signage within the town of Chatham, then expand efforts to include signage at the CCRT Harwich Bicycle Rotary, key Route 6 exits, and bridge approaches to the Cape.

Implementation of Scenario 2 could cost upwards of several million dollars, if FWS decided to construct a brand new and large visitor contact station or purchase a waterfront site. Aside from real estate costs, the other elements of Scenario 2 could be implemented for an investment of $100,000 to $175,000. Note that some costs are one-time capital investments, such as purchase of a 15-passenger van to serve as a shuttle, or contracting for the creation of new metal signs. Because this Scenario includes fewer engineering improvements (e.g., pathways or sidewalks), there are fewer maintenance challenges for the town or MNWR. This scenario is expected to have mixed public approval, with potentially strong support for signage and wayfinding campaigns, and potential controversy associated with acquisition of waterfront property.

Table 16: Summary Scenario 2 - Relocation of Monomoy Visitor Contact Station

SCENARIO 2 ELEMENT	COST	IMPLEMENTATION TIME FRAME	PARTNERSHIPS
Relocate MNWR visitor contact station (including all administrative activities, exhibits, and other services) to downtown Chatham	$400,000 - $1,500,000	LONG: Depends on availability of property and funding PHASES: • Identify suitable, available alternate location • Obtain funding and approval for purchase • Perform construction or other necessary site improvements • Relocate MNWR visitor and administrative functions	Town of Chatham
Add bicycle and pedestrian facilities and amenities at new visitor contact station	$100 to $700 per bike rack (depending on design and number of bikes. Does not include cost of installation) $10,000 to $15,000 per bus shelter (depending on design) $100 to $500 per trash receptacle (more for solar compacting receptacles) Outdoor bulletin boards with traveler information as low as $200; electronic kiosks range from $1,000 to $8,000	MEDIUM: Within 1-2 years PHASES: • Funding • Planning and design • Installation	Town of Chatham
Identify alternate water-based access to Monomoy Islands	$40 to $150 per mooring rental per year	LONG: 1-20 years	Town of Chatham

6. Alternative Transportation Scenarios   Monomoy National Wildlife Refuge Alternative Transportation Study

SCENARIO 2 ELEMENT	COST	IMPLEMENTATION TIME FRAME	PARTNERSHIPS
	$400,000 – $2 million to purchase a waterfront site	PHASES: • Either apply for a town mooring or purchase waterfront property.	
Improve directional signage to MNWR visitor contact station	~$100 for directional or informational signs; several thousand dollars for coordinated wayfinding campaign.	SHORT: within 1 year PHASES: • Select signage designs and locations based on existing planning recommendations • Allocate funding • Install signage	Town of Chatham, Mass Department of Transportation
Add directional and informational signage throughout Chatham	~$100 for directional or informational signs; several thousand dollars for coordinated wayfinding campaign.	MEDIUM: Within 1-2 years PHASES: • Funding • Planning and design • Installation	Town of Chatham, Mass Department of Transportation
Add directional and information signage throughout Cape Cod and along Route 6	~$100 for directional or informational signs; several thousand dollars for coordinated wayfinding campaign.	LONG: Within 5 years PHASES: • Agreement with multiple jurisdictions about signage placement • Funding • Planning and design • Installation	Cape Cod Commission, Mass Department of Transportation, Mass Department of Conservation and Recreation, other towns

6. Alternative Transportation Scenarios   Monomoy National Wildlife Refuge Alternative Transportation Study

SCENARIO 2

ELEMENT	COST	IMPLEMENTATION TIME FRAME	PARTNERSHIPS
Provide a shuttle to the ferry from new downtown visitor contact station	~$30,000 per season for operations and maintenance $50,000 for a 15-passenger van	LONG: Within 5 years or longer PHASES: • Funding • Transit planning • Vehicle purchase • Operations and maintenance • Marketing and promotion	Town of Chatham (?), Rip Ryder, other ferry concessionaire
Improve traveler information on MNWR Web site	$0 - $20,000 depending on scope of changes	SHORT: within 1 year PHASES: • Plan content updates and site improvements • Publish updates	

6.5. Scenario 3: Roadway Safety Improvements

This scenario seeks to provide roadway safety improvements for visitors to MNWR and other popular Chatham destinations. Strategic outcomes and expected impacts include:

- Additional space for parking and travel along the Causeway;
- Improved access for emergency vehicles traveling to/from Morris Island across the Causeway;
- Improved pedestrian safety to access Lighthouse Beach; and
- Reduced confusion/increased awareness of travel options for MNWR and Chatham area visitors.

In this scenario, immediate or "first-level" anticipated impacts include improved roadway safety for visitors to MNWR and Lighthouse Beach. Later ("second-level" or "third-level") impacts can include reduced traffic congestion (?) and increased visitation to MNWR through improved traveler information.

> **SCENARIO 3 INTERVENTIONS:**
>
> Move Causeway fencing to better accommodate parked cars and emergency vehicles
>
> Construct sidewalk between Bridge Street parking areas and Lighthouse Beach
>
> Improve signage and wayfinding
>
> Improve traveler information on the MNWR Website

Description

The sidebar on the right lists the interventions included in Scenario 3. More information is provided in Table 17. This scenario focuses on roadway safety improvements to both MNWR and Lighthouse Beach. The key elements of this scenario are the relocation of the fencing along the Causeway to provide additional space for parking and construction of a sidewalk between the Bridge Street parking area and Lighthouse Beach.

Scenario 3 also includes an enhanced traveler information campaign to assist visitors in accessing MNWR by shuttle, bicycle, foot, or car. A traveler information and outreach campaign could feature printed or web-based information regarding MNWR, as well as general signage improvements. Directions on the MNWR website could be expanded to include how to reach the refuge by bicycle, and detailed information on preferred routes for different modes of transportation. Overall improved signage throughout Cape Cod, in Chatham, and around Morris Island could reduce visitor confusion and facilitate multi-modal access to different locations throughout Chatham and to the refuge.

Discussion

This scenario is designed to meet the project goals of improved safety and improved traveler information regarding access to MNWR, thereby enhancing the visitor experience. Relocation of the fencing along the Causeway to provide additional space for parking would allow additional roadway space for vehicles, bicycles, or pedestrians, and would improve visibility for all roadway users. It would also improve access to Morris Island for emergency vehicles or larger vehicles (e.g., school buses), which currently have difficulty navigating the Causeway when there are many parked vehicles narrowing the roadway. While the town elected not to widen the Causeway in the past, town officials may consider such an alternative at this time, particularly if the relocation of the fencing does not include asphalt paving, but uses a permeable paving material.

A new sidewalk along Bridge Street would serve visitors to Lighthouse Beach, who currently park on Bridge Street and walk, often in the road, to the beach. More detailed surveys and engineering studies are necessary to determine the availability of sufficient roadway right of way for the sidewalk, as well as other key topographical or drainage related issues. An initial review indicates that there may be sufficient right of way on Bridge Street for a sidewalk in addition to the travel lanes; the review assumes, however, that some of the available right of way is used for the parking area, and might not leave enough space for a sidewalk. Increased sidewalk availability is assumed to improve traveler safety and traffic flow. The additional sidewalk would move pedestrians to a dedicated space out of the roadway and improve visibility for oncoming traffic. This intervention would narrow, or appear to narrow the roadway, which could also potentially improve traveler safety by reducing traffic speeds.

While sidewalk construction is not expected to adversely affect traffic flow or safety, crossings along the new facility may present safety concerns. For example, if a sidewalk were constructed on only one side of Bridge Street while visitors were able to park on the other side of the street, then some accommodation would be necessary to allow people to safely cross from their vehicles to access the sidewalk. Allowing pedestrians to cross the road at any point might diminish some of the improvements to safety, visibility, and traffic flow that would be gained by providing a sidewalk on Bridge Street.

Overall, the interventions in this scenario are expected to improve traveler safety. It should be noted that there is no particularly high history of crashes or other traffic incidents on Bridge Street or the Causeway. However, crash data do not capture "near misses" or traveler decisions to drive rather than walk or bicycle because of perceived lack of safety.

This scenario improves roadway safety and the visitor experience, but it does not focus on alternative transportation options. The sidewalk on Bridge Street would be an important facility and would promote pedestrian safety, but it is specifically intended to connect to a parking area, meaning that users of the facility would travel to the area by automobile. Similarly, improved signage and visitor information are important to enhance the visitor experience, but they must be coupled with interventions that encourage the use of other modes, so that they do not merely bring more automobiles to already congested areas. The key roadway safety improvements identified in Scenario 3 are intended for facilities not located within the FWS jurisdiction. FWS could be an important partner in design, implementation, and possibly funding these improvements, even though it cannot initiate project construction. In order to better promote the access goals within this study, FWS might pursue implementation of Scenario 3 in addition to some or all elements of the other scenarios.

Implementation of Scenario 3 is expected to cost $300-400,000, the bulk of which is attributed to the sidewalk construction and engineering ($200,000+), and to the Causeway engineering ($125,000+). These are primarily one-time capital costs, with some ongoing maintenance to be performed by the town or another partner. The costs associated with signage and an information campaign would depend largely on the scope of these interventions. This scenario is expected to have mixed public approval, with support for the safety improvements, concern about right of way and environmental issues related to the construction, and some potential for concerns about aesthetics and visual clutter, related to signage improvements.

6. Alternative Transportation Scenarios   Monomoy National Wildlife Refuge Alternative Transportation Study

Table 17: Summary Scenario 3 - Roadway Safety Improvements

SCENARIO 3 ELEMENT	COST	IMPLEMENTATION TIME FRAME	PARTNERSHIPS
Move Causeway fencing to better accommodate parked cars and emergency vehicles	$125,000 to remove fencing and provide new fencing and stabilization with 10-foot area of crushed stone $5,000 per 1 to 2 years for maintenance and replenishing crushed stone	MEDIUM: Within 1-2 years PHASES: • Funding • Engineering study • Construction	Town of Chatham
Construct sidewalk between Bridge Street parking areas and Lighthouse Beach	~$200,000 for sidewalk and curbing for ~0.5 mile section	MEDIUM: Within 1-2 years PHASES: • Funding • Planning and design • Installation	Town of Chatham
Add directional and informational signage throughout Chatham	~$100 for directional or informational signs; several thousand dollars for coordinated wayfinding campaign.	MEDIUM: Within 1-2 years PHASES: • Funding • Planning and design • Installation	Town of Chatham, Mass Department of Transportation
Add directional and information signage throughout Cape Cod and along Route 6	~$100 for directional or informational signs; several thousand dollars for coordinated wayfinding campaign.	LONG: Within 5 years PHASES: • Agreement with multiple jurisdictions about signage placement • Funding • Planning and design • Installation	Cape Cod Commission, Mass Department of Transportation, Mass Department of Conservation and Recreation, other towns
Improve bicycle route signage	~$100 per sign	MEDIUM: Within 1-2 years	Town of Chatham, Bicycle Commission,

6. Alternative Transportation Scenarios   Monomoy National Wildlife Refuge Alternative Transportation Study

SCENARIO 3

ELEMENT	COST	IMPLEMENTATION TIME FRAME	PARTNERSHIPS
		PHASES: • Funding • Planning and design • Installation	Mass Department of Transportation
Improve traveler information on MNWR website	$0 - $20,000 depending on scope of changes	SHORT: within 1 year PHASES: • Plan content updates and site improvements • Publish updates	

6.6.   Scenario 4: Nonmotorized Transportation Improvements

This scenario seeks to enhance nonmotorized access and improve safety for visitors to MNWR and other popular Chatham destinations. Strategic outcomes and expected impacts include:

- Improved bicycle and pedestrian access and safety to Morris Island and generally around Chatham;

- Increased awareness and information about bicycle and pedestrian access options;

- Additional bicycle parking facilities at priority locations in Chatham; and

- Reduced confusion/increased awareness of travel options to MNWR and Chatham area visitors.

In this scenario, immediate or "first-level" anticipated impacts include improved availability and safety of pedestrian and bicycle facilities. Later ("second-level" or "third-level") impacts include reduced traffic congestion (by encouraging some residents and visitors to travel by foot or bicycle instead of automobile) and increased visitation to MNWR (by improving knowledge of travel options).

> **SCENARIO 4 INTERVENTIONS:**
>
> Create multi-use path on one side of Causeway for bicycles and pedestrians
>
> Provide additional bicycle racks at Visitor Contact Station, Lighthouse Beach, and high priority downtown locations
>
> Paint "Sharrow" or shared lane markings on signed bicycle route for bicycles
>
> Improve signage and wayfinding
>
> Improve traveler information on the

Description

The sidebar at right provides the list of interventions included in Scenario 4. More information is provided in Table 18. This scenario focuses on enhancing nonmotorized – bicycle and pedestrian – access to both MNWR and Lighthouse Beach, through a combination of infrastructure and information improvements. The key elements of the scenario are construction of a multi-use path on one side of the Causeway for bicycle and pedestrian access to MNWR, painted shared lane markings on the signed bicycle route, and additional bicycle parking facilities at key locations throughout Chatham.

Scenario 4 also includes an enhanced traveler information and outreach campaign to assist visitors in accessing MNWR by shuttle, bicycle, foot, or car. The information and outreach campaign could feature printed or web-based information, including improved general signage and information regarding the refuge. Directions on the MNWR Web site could provide routes to the refuge for different modes of transportation. Overall improved signage throughout Cape Cod, in Chatham, and around Morris Island could reduce visitor confusion and facilitate multi-modal travel throughout Chatham and to the refuge.

Discussion

This scenario is designed to meet the project goals of improved safety and alternative transportation access to MNWR, thereby enhancing the visitor experience. The multi-use path on the Causeway would provide a safe, dedicated space for pedestrians and bicyclists along the narrow stretch of road from the mainland to Morris

Island. While current volumes of pedestrian and bicycle traffic along this roadway are relatively low, the provision of a dedicated path would alleviate concerns about available space and visibility, and may encourage more residents and visitors to walk or cycle along the Causeway.

Shared lane markings along the length of the signed bicycle route would serve two primary purposes – they would provide important directional information to cyclists indicating the preferred route, and they would also remind both drivers and cyclists of the need to allow adequate space for the cyclist. This could mean drivers taking more room on the road to pass cyclists, or accommodating cyclists' use of the full lane when necessary. While such markings are typically intended for wider roadways, there are examples of their use on narrow roadways in Massachusetts, primarily in urban areas.

Overall, the interventions in this scenario are expected to improve traveler safety and highlight bicycle and pedestrian safety. It should be noted that there is not a significant history of crashes or other traffic incidents on the Causeway or bicycle crashes on the signed route. However, crash data do not capture "near misses" or traveler decisions to drive rather than walk or bicycle because of perceived lack of safety.

Construction of the Causeway path is not expected to adversely affect traffic flow or safety, though there may be concerns related to pedestrians or cyclists crossing the Causeway to access the path. Visitors traveling toward MNWR from the mainland would have to cross Morris Island Road to access the head of the path. Such a crossing might justify some sort of signage or signalization to alert motorists to the presence of pedestrians and cyclists, and direct users of the path to cross at the preferred location. It might also be valuable to consider allowing a crossing point along the path for users to access the water on the other side of the roadway for shell-fishing. Without planned crossing points, pedestrians may attempt cross the road at random points, diminishing improvements to safety, visibility, and traffic flow on the Causeway.

While this scenario expands alternative transportation options, its potential for traffic congestion reduction may be limited: there is no data on demand for enhanced bicycle and pedestrian facilities, thus making it unclear how many visitors or residents would switch modes. Also, there is no guarantee that the other visitor destinations would be well served by nonmotorized infrastructure, which could limit to the number of visitors who travel by foot or bicycle. In response to these limitations, this scenario promotes overall improvements in the Chatham area, providing more options in general for cycling and walking. Non-infrastructure amenities such as bicycle parking also facilitate the decision to cycle instead of drive; cyclists must feel assured of safe and convenient bicycle storage if they choose to travel by that mode. Safe and convenient bicycle parking could potentially encourage some visitors to travel by bicycle instead of automobile, given the difficulties in finding automobile parking in downtown Chatham.

This scenario does not provide an exhaustive list of nonmotorized improvements in Chatham, but highlights some of the priority elements related to access to MNWR. While Scenario 4 promotes a combination of infrastructure and information that complement each other, not all elements would have to be implemented simultaneously. FWS and local stakeholders could also identify other nonmotorized improvements to promote access within Chatham and to MNWR. FWS and local stakeholders should coordinate with the National Park Service, which has also undertaken a study across Cape Cod to identify bicycle facility and signage priorities.

Implementation of Scenario 4 is expected to cost $100,000-125,000, nearly all of which is attributed to the path construction and engineering ($85,000). These are primarily one-time capital costs, with some ongoing maintenance to be performed by the town or another partner. The costs associated with signage and an information campaign would depend largely on the scope of these campaigns. This scenario is expected to have mixed public approval, with strong support for the multi-use path, and some potential for concerns about aesthetics and visual clutter, related to signage improvements.

6. Alternative Transportation Scenarios   Monomoy National Wildlife Refuge Alternative Transportation Study

Table 18: Summary Scenario 4 - Nonmotorized Transportation Improvements

ELEMENT	COST	IMPLEMENTATION TIME FRAME	PARTNERSHIPS
Create multi-use path on one side of Causeway for bicycles and pedestrians	$85,000 for planning, designing, and constructing 8-foot crushed stone path $1-2,000 per year for maintenance	LONG: Within 5 years PHASES: • Funding • Planning and design • Environmental review and permitting • Construction	Town of Chatham, Mass Department of Transportation (?)
Paint "Sharrow" or shared lane markings on signed bicycle route for bicycles	Pavement markings for bicycles from $50-$300 per symbol	MEDIUM: Within 1-2 years PHASES: • Funding • Planning and design • Installation	Bicycle route signage or lane markings would require Town of Chatham approval on local roads. State roadway markings would require Mass DOT approval.
Provide additional bicycle racks at headquarters/visitor contact station, Lighthouse Beach, and high priority downtown locations	$100 to $700 per bike rack (depending on design and number of bikes. Does not include cost of installation)	MEDIUM: Within 1-2 years PHASES: • Funding • Planning and siting • Installation • Maintenance	Town of Chatham, NPS
Add directional and informational signage throughout Chatham	~$100 for directional or informational signs; several thousand dollars for coordinated wayfinding campaign.	MEDIUM: Within 1-2 years PHASES: • Funding • Planning and design • Installation	Town of Chatham, Mass Department of Transportation
Add directional and information signage throughout Cape Cod and along Route 6	~$100 for directional or informational signs; several thousand dollars for	LONG: Within 5 years PHASES:	Cape Cod Commission, Mass Department of Transportation, Mass Department of Conservation and

6. Alternative Transportation Scenarios   Monomoy National Wildlife Refuge Alternative Transportation Study

ELEMENT	COST	IMPLEMENTATION TIME FRAME	PARTNERSHIPS
	coordinated wayfinding campaign.	• Agreement with multiple jurisdictions about signage placement • Funding • Planning and design • Installation	Recreation, other towns
Improve bicycle route signage	~$100 per sign	MEDIUM: Within 1-2 years PHASES: • Funding • Planning and design • Installation	Town of Chatham, Bicycle Commission, Mass Department of Transportation
Improve traveler information on MNWR website	$0 - $20,000 depending on scope of changes	SHORT: within 1 year PHASES: • Plan content updates and site improvements • Publish updates	

7. NEXT STEPS

The MNWR Alternative Transportation Study provides a wide-range of information and potential transportation-related interventions that FWS could pursue to improve access to and information about MNWR. While this study does not make specific recommendations for what FWS should implement, it provides FWS with the tools to make informed decisions on how to meet its goals through pursuing alternative transportation improvements.

One major component of this study that could inform next steps is the partnership assessment. While several of the activities detailed in the study could be undertaken by FWS alone, most would require cooperation and partnership with other local, regional, state, Federal, and non-governmental entities. If FWS hopes to pursue any of the interventions detailed in this study, it would benefit from reaching out to the potential partners detailed in the partnership assessment chapter to establish stronger partnerships. In doing so, FWS would increase the potential success for implementation of any alternative transportation intervention.

This study also provides FWS with information on cost, implementation considerations, and potential unintended consequences of each of the interventions and groupings of interventions. This information can be used to guide decisions about which interventions FWS pursues; however, full implementation will require additional study into specific engineering, cost and environmental considerations.

This study provides information about potential funding sources that could support implementation of some or all of the interventions and scenarios in APPENDIX L.

The information in this study will provide important background information for FWS as it moves forward to develop the Comprehensive Conservation Plan (CCP) for the Monomoy National Wildlife Refuge. FWS may extract or reference helpful sections of this study within the body of the CCP as desired.

The MNWR Alternative Transportation Study explores the range of possible alternative transportation interventions, and narrows the list to those that would be beneficial to MNWR and the town of Chatham. From this list, and associated information, FWS should be able to identify projects to meet its goals, and begin to explore methods of implementation.

8. REFERENCES

(TAG), Interagency Transportation Assistance Group. (2007). *Transportation Observations, Considerations, and Recommendations for the Monomoy National Wildlife Refuge.* Cambridge: The U.S. Department of Transportation John A. Volpe National Transportation Systems Center.

Cape Cod Commission. (2007). *Cape Cod 2007 Regional Transportation Plan.* Barnstable County: Cape Cod Commission.

Cape Cod Commission. (2008). *Cape Cod Traffic Counting: Chatham Traffic Counts: 1998-2008.* Cape Cod Commission.

Cape Cod Commission. (2008, February). Cape Collects $12 Million in State Room Tax. Barnstable, Massachusetts, USA.

Cape Cod Commission, Cape Cod Economic Development Council. (2005). *Cape Cod Region Comprehensive Economic Development Strategy.* Cape Cod Commission.

Coldwell Banker. (n.d.). *Stage Harbor Real Estate.* Retrieved December 9, 2009, from Stage Harbor Real Estate: http://www.mlscapecod.net/Stage-Harbor-Real-Estate/index.cfm

Dero Bike Rack Co. (n.d.). Retrieved December 9, 2009, from Dero Bike Racks: http://www.dero.com/products/zap/

Division of Economics, U.S. Fish and Wildlife Service. (2007). *Banking on Nature 2006: The Economic Benefits to Local Communities of National Wildlife Refuge Visitation.* U.S. Fish and Wildlife Service.

Gate Depot. (n.d.). *Gate Depot.* Retrieved December 9, 2009, from http://www.gatedepot.com/index.php

Gate-Opener. (n.d.). Retrieved December 9, 2009, from Gate-Opener: http://www.gate-opener.com/

Lake Superior Duluth. (n.d.). *Pervious Pavement.* Retrieved December 9, 2009, from streams.org: http://lakesuperiorstreams.org/stormwater/toolkit/paving.html

LoopNet. (n.d.). Retrieved December 9, 2009, from LoopNet: http://www.loopnet.com/

Massachusetts Department of Environmental Protection. (2003). *Source Water Assessment and Protection (SWAP) Report for Chatham Water Department.* Massachusetts Department of Environmental Protection.

Massachusetts Department of Housing and Community Development . (n.d.). *Town of Chatham.* Retrieved December 9, 2009, from Chatham Community Profile: http://www.mass.gov/?pageID=mg2localgovccpage&L=3&L0=Home&L1=State+Government&L2=Local+Government&sid=massgov2&selectCity=Chatham

MassGIS. (n.d.). *MassGIS.* Retrieved 12 04, 2009, from http://www.mass.gov/mgis/

Multiple Listing Service. (n.d.). *Multiple Listing Service*. Retrieved December 9, 2009, from
http://www.mls.com/

National Park Service. (1998). *Cape Cod National Seashore General Management Plan*. National Park
Service.

Pedestrian and Bicycling Information Center. (n.d.). *Cost Demand Benefits Analysis Tool*. Retrieved
December 9, 2009, from bicyclinginfo.org: http://www.bicyclinginfo.org/bikecost/

Sportworks. (n.d.). *Sportworks Bicycle and Transit Solutions*. Retrieved December 9, 2009, from
http://www.sportworks.com/

State of California, Business, Transportation and Housing Agency, Department of Transportation. (2008).
2008 Contract Cost Data. Sacramento: Caltrans.

The Stormwater Manager's Resource Center. (n.d.). *Stormwater Management Fact Sheet: Porous
Pavement*. Retrieved December 9, 2009, from The Stormwater Manager's Resource Center:
http://www.stormwatercenter.net/Assorted%20Fact%20Sheets/Tool6_Stormwater_Practices/Infiltration%
20Practice/Porous%20Pavement.htm

Town of Chatham. (2003). *Chatham, Massachusetts Long Range Comprehensive Plan*. Chatham: Town
of Chatham.

Town of Chatham. (n.d.). *Harbormaster*. Retrieved December 9, 2009, from Town of Chatham,
Massachusetts: http://www.town.chatham.ma.us/Public_Documents/ChathamMA_Harbor/index

U.S. Census 2000. (2000). MCD/County-To-MCD/County Worker Flow Files.

U.S. Census 2000. (2000). Summary File 3

U.S. Census 2000. (2004). U.S. Census Bureau Population Estimates.

U.S. Census 2000. (2000). Zip Code Business Patterns.

U.S. Fish and Wildlife Service. (n.d.). Retrieved December 9, 2009, from U.S. Fish and Wildlife Service:
http://www.fws.gov/

Victoria Transport Policy Institute. (2009). *Transportation Cost and Benefit Analysis, Techniques,
Estimates and Implications, Second Edition*. Victoria : Victoria Transport Policy Institute.

APPENDIX A. List of Acronyms

ACEC	Areas of Critical Environmental Concern
ATPPL	Alternative Transportation in Parks and Public Lands
ATS	Alternative Transportation Study
CACO	Cape Cod National Seashore
CCC	Cape Cod Commission
CCP	Comprehensive Conservation Plan
CCRT	Cape Cod Rail Trail
CCRTA	Cape Cod Regional Transit Authority
CPD	Chatham Police Department
DCR	Department of Conservation and Recreation
DPW	Department of Public Works
FTA	Federal Transit Administration
FWS	Fish and Wildlife Service
IBA	Important Bird Area
ITS	Intelligent Transportation Systems
MassDOT	Massachusetts Department of Transportation
MNWR	Monomoy National Wildlife Refuge
NEPA	National Environmental Policy Act
NPS	National Parks Service
NSFHWR	National Survey of Fishing, Hunting, and Wildlife-Associated Recreation
RAPP	Refuge Annual Performance Plan
ROW	Right of Way
SUP	Special Use Permit
TAG	Transportation Advisory Group
USCG	United States Coast Guard
WHSRN	Western Hemispheric Shorebird Reserve Network Site

APPENDIX B. August 2008 Public Meeting Notes & Materials

MONOMOY NATIONAL WILDLIFE REFUGE
Alternative Transportation Study (2008-09)

What is the Monomoy National Wildlife Refuge Alternative Transportation Study?

The purpose of the study is to gather information, identify transportation issues, and develop and analyze possible alternatives that can be considered for implementation by the Monomoy National Wildlife Refuge and the U.S. Fish & Wildlife Service. Goals include:

- Studying alternatives to improve access to the refuge and Chatham area (such as shuttles, vans, and existing FlexRoute service);
- Exploring opportunities for partnerships with local public agencies and businesses;
- Coordinating with the Refuge's "Comprehensive Conservation Plan" (CCP) effort;
- Examining future funding needs and potential funding sources for implementation.

What is the timeline and schedule for the project?

The project began in late Summer 2008 and should be completed by Summer 2009. Some components of the project include:

Analyze conditions and transportation data.	Gather opinions and discuss topics with the public.	Develop and analyze potential alternatives.	Review implementation considerations and write research

→ SUMMER 2008 ———→ FALL/WINTER 2009 ———→ SUMMER 2009

How can the public become involved?

Public input is important to the success of this study. There will be opportunities for the public to attend meetings, share ideas, and submit comments.

Questions, comments, and suggestions can be submitted at any time to:
MonomoyTraffic@gmail.com

How will updates and results be shared?

The research study should be concluded in Summer 2009. Updates and results may appear:

ON THE WEB   IN PRESENTATIONS   IN THE NEWS   IN A FINAL REPORT

Summary of Meeting Notes

Problems / Concerns	Potential Solutions
• Roadway Maintenance on Morris Island (responsibility of residents, concern over large vehicles) • Number of cars accessing Morris Island • Need for access possibilities by other modes (e.g. water)	• Widen causeway shoulder (not paved, e.g. move the fencing) • Utilize other parking facilities in town (e.g. high school) and have a shuttle bring visitors to the headquarters/visitor contact station • Develop and/or sign a bike route to Morris Island • Expanded ferry service to Monomoy Islands and/or Morris Island (parking and docking sites not identified) • Restrict or eliminate parking at Morris Island (and enforcement) • Charge for parking at Morris Island • Shuttle vehicle from off-site parking to Morris Island • Find and use an alternate site for refuge visitor contact station • Off-site variable message signage (location not identified) to alert visitors that Morris Island parking lot is full
• Schoolbus access to Morris Island	• School groups use vans
• Accessibility issues (e.g. for people with disabilities)	• Widen and maintain footpath • Find acceptable ADA alternative pathways
• Want more information on who accesses refuge (residents vs. tourists, etc.)	• License plate survey (and check for town stickers or check zip codes)
• Bridge Street is narrow, parking on both sides creates safety concern	• Restrictions on parking (e.g., one side only) • Parking enforcement • Widen roadway for more formal parking area • Widen to allow for angle parking • Charge for parking • Park & ride (free or charge?) • Make roadway one-way traffic • Allow vehicle access to Lighthouse Beach
• Other	• Improve signage and paths for kayakers to better indicate preferred route along Causeway • Find alternate docking site for ferries • Duck Boats

Other Considerations:
- Parking on the Causeway has been less of a problem this year than in past years
- Chatham traffic and parking problems are only really bad for 2-3 months per year. Solutions should either be seasonal or an acceptable year round solution (e.g., perhaps road widening is not desirable for the full year)
- Off-site parking lots for a shuttle service would most likely have to be at schools (using parking lots near downtown would exacerbate the downtown parking crunch)
- The study needs to clarify the connection between Monomoy access and Lighthouse Beach/Bridge Street issues, and also clarify connection between Monomoy access and general town-wide transportation issues
- Concern that improving access to Morris Island will also increase traffic congestion – hence the need for alternate modes of access
- Alternatives will need to consider current as well as future refuge needs
- Is there a desired level of refuge visitation? Is there a point at which more visitation threatens the wildlife and/or is unsustainable to Morris Island and the transportation infrastructure? What is the carrying capacity of the Refuge Center?

APPENDIX C. Partnership Assessment Matrix

Partner Activities

PARTNER ACTIVITIES

Partner Organization	Type of Organization / Subgroup	O&M Bike Racks	O&M Parking Areas	O&M Bus Shelters	O&M Shuttle Service	O&M Traveler Info (kiosk, etc.)	Web-based	Print Media	Broadcast Media	Email/ Mailings	Traveler Information	Liaison to other groups / govs	Collect /provide data	Cap. Bike Racks	Cap. Bus Shelters	Cap. Vehicles	Cap. Traveler Information	Staff Support	Volunteer Support	Discounted Tickets	Shuttle Service	Ferry Service	Tours	Other
Cape Cod Commission	Regional Land Use and Trans. Planning						X			X	X	X	X					X						
Cape Cod Regional Transit Authority	Local transit agency			X	X		X				X				?	?	?							
FWS Region 5	Refuge Roads Program Manager	?	?				?							?	?	?	?	X						
Monomoy Island Ferry (Rip Ryder)	Ferry Service to Islands		?				X				X									X		X		
National Park Service, Cape Cod National Seashore	Manager of Cape Cod Coastline						X				X		X	?		?	X			X				
Outermost Harbor Marine	Ferry Service to Islands		?				X				X									X		X		
MA Department of Cons. and Recreation	State government					X	X			X	X	?	X				X		X					
Town of Chatham	Chatham Public Schools		X	X		X	X			X		?							?					
Town of Chatham	Planning Department						X			X	X	X	X	?	?	?	?	X						

Appendix C. Partnership Assessment Matrix   **Monomoy National Wildlife Refuge Alternative Transportation Study**

Partner Organization	Type of Organization / Subgroup	Bike Racks	Parking Areas	Bus Shelters	Shuttle Service	Traveler Info (kiosk, etc.)	Web-based	Print Media	Broadcast Media	Email/ Mailings	Traveler Information	Liaison to other groups / govs	Collect /provide data	Bike Racks	Bus Shelters	Vehicles	Traveler Information	Staff Support	Volunteer Support	Discounted Tickets	Shuttle Service	Ferry Service	Tours	Other
Town of Chatham	Bikeways Commission	?				?	X			X	X	?	?						X				?	
Town of Chatham	Police Department		?			?					?		X											Enforce parking restrictions
Town of Chatham	Town Landing Officer		?																					Identify/provide dock space for MNWR ferries
Cape Cod Chronicle	Local Newspaper							X			X													
Cape Cod Times	Local Newspaper							X			X													
Radio WQRC	Radio Station								X		X													
Chatham Chamber of Commerce	Local business association					?						X	X							?				
Chatham Council on Aging	Local civic organization				?											?			?		?			Coordinate with existing paratransit
Chatham Historical Society	Local civic organization					?	?			?	?								?				?	
Town of Chatham	Harbor Master											X	?											Could provide aid to ferry services
Mass Audubon, Wellfleet Bay Wildlife Sanctuary	Civic organization						X			X													?	Shuttle from Welfleet Sanctuatry
Coastal Waterbird	Mass Audubon						X			X		X											?	
USCG												X	?										?	Provide aid to Ferry

MNWR Activities

MNWR ACTIVITIES

Partner Organization	Type of Organization / Subgroup	O&M: Bike Racks	O&M: Parking Areas	O&M: Bus Shelters	O&M: Shuttle Service	O&M: Traveler Information (kiosk, etc.)	Outreach: Web-based	Outreach: Email/Mailings	Outreach: Traveler Information	Outreach: Liaison to other groups / governments	Outreach: Collect / provide data	Capital: Bike Racks	Capital: Bus Shelters	Capital: Vehicles	Capital: Traveler Information	In-Kind: Staff support	In-Kind: Volunteer support	In-Kind: Discounted Tickets	Other
Cape Cod Commission	Regional Land Use and Trans. Planning										X	?	?	?		X			
Cape Cod Regional Transit Authority	Local transit agency					X	X	X				X	X	X	X	X			
FWS Region 5	Refuge Roads Program Manager					?					?					X	?		
Monomoy Island Ferry (Rip Ryder)	Ferry Service to Islands		X			X	X		X		?	X			X				
National Park Service, Cape Cod National Seashore	Manager of Cape Cod Coastline						X		X		X	?	?	?	?			X	
Outermost Harbor Marine	Ferry Service to Islands		X			X						X	?		X				
MA Department of Conservation and Recreation	State government						?	?	?			?		?	?				
Town of Chatham	Chatham Public Schools						?	?	?		?	X	X		X	X		?	
Town of Chatham	Planning Department						?	?	?		?	X	X	?	X	X			
Town of Chatham	Bikeways Commission	?					?	?	?			X		X	?	X			
Town of Chatham	Police Department																		
Town of Chatham	Town Landing Officer		?																
Cape Cod Chronicle	Local Newspaper								X	X	X								
Cape Cod Times	Local Newspaper								X	X	X								
Radio WQRC	Radio Station						?		?		X								
Chatham Chamber of Commerce	Local business association								X	X	X							X	
Chatham Council on Aging	Local civic organization							X					?						
Chatham Historical Society	Local civic organization						?				?								

Partner Organization	Type of Organization / Subgroup	Bike Racks	Parking Areas	Bus Shelters	Shuttle Service	Traveler Information (kiosk, etc.)	Web-based	Email/ Mailings	Traveler Information	Liaison to other groups / governments	Collect / provide data	Bike Racks	Bus Shelters	Vehicles	Traveler Information	Staff support	Volunteer support	Discounted Tickets	Other
Town of Chatham	Harbor Master						?		?		?			?					Also maybe Docking area for rescue boats
Mass Audubon, Wellfleet Bay Wildlife Sanctuary	Civic organization						?		?										
Coastal Waterbird	Mass Audubon						?		?										
USCG										X	X								Docking area for rescue boats

Contact List

First Name	Last Name	Title	Affiliation	Address	Phone	Fax	Email
Tim	Wood	Editor	Cape Cod Chronicle		508-945-2220		twood@capecodchronicle.com
Clay	Schofield	Transportation Engineer	Cape Cod Commission	3225 Main St. PO BOX 226, Barnstable, MA 02630-0226	508-362-3828	508-362-3136	cschofield@capecodcommission.org
Robin	Lord	Reporter	Cape Cod Times	319 Main St., Hyannis, MA, 02601	508-775-1200		rlord@capecodonline.com
Doug	Blackwell	Resident	Chatham				dblackwell2004@comcast.net
Stephen	Buckley	Resident	Chatham		508-945-0518		mailto:msbuckley@igc.org
Tina & Bob	Cantor	Resident	Chatham				rcantor@emersonhosp.org
Don	Lynch	Resident	Chatham				
Pat	Thornton	Resident	Chatham				
Jesse	Decker		Chatham Bars Inn	297 Shore Road, Chatham MA 02633	508-945-6803		
Lisa	Franz	President	Chatham Chamber of Commerce	2377 Main Street Chatham MA 02633	508-945-5199	508-430-7919	mailto:lisa@chathaminfo.com
Ellen	Ford	Director	Chatham Council on Aging	193 Stony Hill Road, Chatham MA 02633	508-945-5190		phoerner@chatham-ma.gov
Jeff	Colby	Superintendent	Chatham DPW	549 Main Street, Chatham MA 02633			jcolby@chatham-ma.gov
Heather	McGrath	President	Chatham Merchants Association	2377 Main Street Chatham MA 02633	508-945-5199		heather@simplerpleasures.com
Dr. Mary Ann	Lanzo	Superintendent	Chatham Public Schools	425 Crowell Rd., Chatham MA 02633	508-945-5130	508-945-5133	mlanzo@chatham.k12.ma.us
David	Taylor		Chatham Rotary Club	http://www.chathamrotary.org			davidtaylor44@comcast.net
Barbara	Waters	Teacher	Chatham Public Schools	425 Crowell Rd., Chatham MA 02633	508-945-5130	508-945-5133	bwaters14@verizon.net
Ron	Bergstrom	Advisory Board Chair	Chatham Selectmen, CCRTA	549 Main Street, Chatham, MA 02633	508 945-5100		ronbergstrom@comcast.net
Tom	Eagle	Deputy Refuge Complex Manager	Eastern Massachusetts NWR Complex	Wikis Way, Morris Island, Chatham MA	508-945-0594	508-945-9559	Thomas_Eagle@fws.gov
Libby	Herland	Refuge Complex Manager	Eastern Massachusetts NWR Complex	73 Weir Hill Road, Sudbury, MA 01776	978-443-4661	978-443-2898	Libby_Herland@fws.gov
Carl	Melberg	Refuge Planner	Eastern Massachusetts NWR Complex	73 Weir Hill Road, Sudbury, MA 01776	978-443-4661	978-443-2898	Carl_Melberg@fws.gov
Sue	Fuller	GIS Specialist /	FWS Realty Office	300 Westgate Center	413-253-8533		sue_fuller@fws.gov

Appendix C. Partnership Assessment Matrix   **Monomoy National Wildlife Refuge Alternative Transportation Study**

First Name	Last Name	Title	Affiliation	Address	Phone	Fax	Email
John	Sauer	Biologist		Drive Hadley, MA 01035			john_sauer@fws.gov
Rick	Schauffler	Refuge Roads Program Manager	FWS Region 5	300 Westgate Center Drive Hadley, MA 01035	413-253-8787		rick_schauffler@fws.gov
Charles	Fuller	GIS Specialist / Biologist	Great Bay NWR	c/o 6 Plum Island Tpke., Newburyport, MA 01950	603-431-3898		
Marcia	Fuller	Resident	Morris Island				
Sanford	Roth	Resident	Morris Island				siroth@northwestern.edu
Joe	Sammartino	Resident	Morris Island				
Joan	Caefer	President	Quitnesset neighborhood group	24 Tilipi Run, Chatham MA 02633	508-945-0502		joe@bostonhotel.com
Ray	Caefer	Resident	Stage Island				jcaefer@comcast.net
William	Hinchey	Resident	Stage Island				rcaefer@comcast.net
Ted	Keon	Town Manager	Town of Chatham	549 Main Street, Chatham MA 02633	(508)-945-5100	508-945-3550	lsmulligan@chatham-ma.gov
Mark	Pawlina	Director of Coastal Resources	Town of Chatham	549 Main Street, Chatham MA 02633	508-945-5176		
Lynn	Thatcher	Chief of Police	Town of Chatham	127 Depot Rd., Chatham MA 02633	508-945-1213	508-945-2791	mpawlina@chatham-ma.gov
Bob	Walsh	Assistant Planner	Town of Chatham	261 George Ryder Rd., Chatham MA 02633	508-945-5168	508-945-5163	lthatcher@chatham-ma.gov
Terry	Whalen	Town Landing Officer	Town of Chatham	549 Main Street, Chatham MA 02633			
John	Cauble	Principal Planner	Town of Chatham	261 George Ryder Rd., Chatham MA 02633	508-945-5160	508-945-5163	twhalen@chatham-ma.gov
Cathy	Schaeffer	Captain	Town of Chatham Police Department	127 Depot Road, Chatham, MA 02633	508-945-1213	508-945-2791	jdcauble@chatham-ma.gov
Kate	Iaquinto	Parking Clerk	Town of Chatham Police Department	PO Box 1347 West Chatham, MA 02669	508-328-5918	508-945-3550	
Jen	Yantachka		USFWS - Monomoy	Wikis Way, Morris Island, Chatham MA	508-945-0594	508-945-9559	Kate_Iaquinto@fws.gov
Keith	Lincoln		USFWS - Monomoy	Wikis Way, Morris Island, Chatham MA	508-945-0594	508-945-9559	jen.yantachka@gmail.com
		Monomoy Island Ferry	Monomoy Island Ferry		508-237-0420		KeithLincoln@comcast.net

APPENDIX D. Scenario Summary Matrix

ELEMENT		Scenario 1 Satellite parking and transit service	Scenario 2 Relocated MNWR visitor contact station	Scenario 3 Roadway safety improvements	Scenario 4 Nonmotorized transportation improvements
1	Identify/secure satellite parking location	X			
2	Use variable message signs at new/redesigned intersection to direct visitors to satellite parking	X			
3	Operate shuttle service to MNWR (and other destinations in Chatham) from satellite parking	X			
4	Provide bicycle facilities/amenities at shuttle stops	X			
5	Provide a shuttle to the ferry from new downtown visitor contact station		X		
6	Install pedestrian improvements at Main St. /Queen Anne Rd. rotary and shuttle stops	X			
7	Implement parking restrictions at headquarters/visitor contact station	X			
8	Improve directional signage to MNWR headquarters/visitor contact station		X		X
9	Add directional and informational signage throughout Chatham	X	X	X	X

Prepared by the U.S. DOT Volpe Center

		Scenario 1	Scenario 2	Scenario 3	Scenario 4
10	Improve bicycle route signage	X		X	X
11	Add directional and information signage throughout Cape Cod and along Route 6	X	X	X	X
12	Relocate MNWR visitor contact station (including all administrative activities, exhibits, and other services) to downtown Chatham		X		
13	Add bicycle and pedestrian facilities and amenities at new visitor contact station		X		
14	Move Causeway fencing to better accommodate parked cars and emergency vehicles			X	
15	Create multi-use path on one side of Causeway for bicycles and pedestrians				X
16	Provide additional bicycle racks at headquarters/visitor contact station, Lighthouse Beach, and high priority downtown locations				X
17	Construct sidewalk between Bridge Street parking areas and Lighthouse Beach			X	
18	Paint "Sharrow" or shared lane markings on signed bicycle route for bicycles				X
19	Improve traveler information on MNWR website	X	X	X	X
20	Identify alternate ferry dock space		X		

APPENDIX E. Shuttle Operations and Costs

Assumptions:

- Hourly operating (and service) cost: $65
- Dwell time at each stop: 45 seconds
- Travel speeds are based on 150% of posted roadway speed
- Note that the service and cost estimates do not include housing the vehicles or travel time between garage and beginning/end of route

Chatham - MNWR Shuttle Route – Loop
Number of stops: 9

	Distance (miles)	Average Speed (mph)	Estimated Run Time (Min)	Estimated Dwell Time (Min)	Assumed Layover Time (Min)	Total Running Time (Min)
Weekday	7.7	13	34	7	5	46
Saturday	7.7	13	34	7	5	46
Sunday	7.7	13	34	7	5	46

Type of Service	Hours of Operation			Days of Operation	Weeks of Operation	Assumed Running Time (Min)	Desired Headway (Min)	Number of Vehicles	Weekly Service Hours	Annual Service Hours	Annual Service Cost
	Begin	End	Total								
Weekday	8.00	22.00	14	5	14	46	20	3	210	2940	$191,100
Saturday	8.00	22.00	14	1	20	46	20	3	42	840	$54,600
Sunday	8.00	20.00	12	1	20	46	20	3	36	720	$46,800
							Total		288	4500	$292,500

Chatham - MNWR Shuttle Route – Linear
Number of stops: 14

	Distance (miles)	Average Speed (mph)	Estimated Run Time (Min)	Estimated Dwell Time (Min)	Assumed Layover Time (Min)	Total Running Time (Min)
Weekday	7.2	12	36	11	5	52
Saturday	7.2	12	36	11	5	52
Sunday	7.2	12	36	11	5	52

Type of Service	Hours of Operation			Days of Operation	Weeks of Operation	Assumed Running Time (Min)	Desired Headway (Min)	Number of Vehicles	Weekly Service Hours	Annual Service Hours	Annual Service Cost
	Begin	End	Total								
Weekday	8.00	22.00	14	5	14	52	20	3	210	2940	$191,100
Saturday	8.00	22.00	14	1	20	52	20	3	42	840	$54,600
Sunday	8.00	20.00	12	1	20	52	20	3	36	720	$46,800
								Total	288	4500	$292,500

APPENDIX F. Scenario Cost Estimates

ID	Element	Cost Range	Unit Cost	# Units	Total Capital Cost	Additional Costs (annual)	Notes	Scenario 1	Scenario 2	Scenario 3	Scenario 4
1	Identify/secure satellite parking location	Unknown					Costs for using satellite parking are unknown	X			
2	Use variable message signs at new/redesigned intersection to direct visitors to satellite parking	$5,000 to $20,000	$15,000	3	$45,000			X			
3	Operate shuttle service to MNWR (and other destinations in Chatham) from satellite parking	$15,000 to $150,000 per vehicle	$50,000	3	$150,000	$300,000	Additional costs for shuttle operations and maintenance	X			
4		$100 to $700 per rack	$600	3	$1,800			X			
4	Provide bicycle facilities/amenities at shuttle stops	$10,000 to $15,000 per bus shelter	$10,000	4	$40,000			X			
4		$100 to $500 for trash receptacles	$500	4	$2,000			X			
4		$200 to $8,000 for outdoor information kiosks	$500	4	$2,000			X			
5	Provide a shuttle to the ferry from new downtown visitor contact station	$15,000 to $150,000 per vehicle	$50,000	1	$50,000	$30,000	Additional costs for shuttle operations and maintenance		X		

ID	Element	Cost Range	Unit Cost	# Units	Total Capital Cost	Additional Costs (annual)	Notes	Scenario 1	Scenario 2	Scenario 3	Scenario 4
6	Install pedestrian improvements at and around shuttle stops	$2,000 to $4,000 for user activated signals	$3,000	2	$6,000			X			
6		$60 to $80 per foot of sidewalk construction					It is unknown at this time if sidewalk construction will be necessary	X			
7	Implement parking restrictions at headquarters/visitor contact station	$0 to $20,000	$1,000	1	$1,000			X			
8	Improve directional signage to MNWR headquarters/visitor contact station	~$100 per sign	$100	4	$400		This does not include costs for installing and regular maintenance of the signs. This might be contracted, done in-house, or accomplished through a partnership. This estimate also does not include a coordinated campaign or strategy for signage.	X	X	X	X
9	Add directional and informational signage throughout Chatham	~$100 per sign	$100	6	$600			X	X	X	X
10	Improve bicycle route signage	~$100 per sign	$100	10	$1,000			X	X	X	X
11	Add directional and information signage throughout Cape Cod and along Route 6	~$100 per sign	$100	6	$600			X	X	X	X
12	Relocate MNWR visitor contact station (including all administrative activities, exhibits, and other services) to downtown Chatham	$400,000 to $2,000,000 for property acquisition (more for area closer to downtown or with waterfront access)	$1,000,000	1	$1,000,000		This applies only to land acquisition - not to demolishing, renovating, building a new building, or other costs for relocating activities		X		
12		Parking lot construction - $200 annual maintenance per space	$5,000	100	$500,000	$20,000	Additional costs for annual maintenance		X		

Appendix F. Scenario Cost Estimates   **Monomoy National Wildlife Refuge Alternative Transportation Study**

ID	Element	Cost Range	Unit Cost	# Units	Total Capital Cost	Additional Costs (annual)	Notes	Scenario 1	Scenario 2	Scenario 3	Scenario 4
13	Add bicycle and pedestrian facilities and amenities at new visitor contact station (list of amenities is not exhaustive)	$100 to $700 per rack	$700	1	$700		Does not include costs for shipping, installation, or regular maintenance. These might need to be contracted or might be able to partner or use in-house resources		X		
13		$10,000 to $15,000 per bus shelter	$10,000	1	$10,000				X		
13		$100 to $500 for trash receptacles	$500	2	$1,000				X		
13		$200 to $8,000 for outdoor information kiosks	$500	1	$500				X		
14	Move Causeway fencing to better accommodate parked cars and emergency vehicles	$125,000 for fencing removal and construction, stabilization	$125,000	1	$125,000	$5,000	Additional costs for annual maintenance			X	
15	Create multi-use path on one side of Causeway for bicycles and pedestrians	$85,000 for fencing removal and construction, stabilization	$85,000	1	$85,000	$2,000	Additional costs for annual maintenance				X
16	Provide additional bicycle racks at headquarters/visitor contact station, Lighthouse Beach, and high priority downtown locations	$100 to $700 per rack	$600	3	$1,800		Does not include costs for shipping, installation, or regular maintenance. These might need to be contracted or might be able to partner or use in-house resources				X
17	Construct sidewalk between Bridge Street parking areas and Lighthouse Beach	$70 per linear foot	$70	2952	$206,640					X	
18	Paint "Sharrow" or shared lane markings on signed bicycle route for bicycles	$100 per marking	$100	150	$15,000						X

Appendix F. Scenario Cost Estimates   Monomoy National Wildlife Refuge Alternative Transportation Study

ID	Element	Cost Range	Unit Cost	# Units	Total Capital Cost	Additional Costs (annual)	Notes	Scenario 1	Scenario 2	Scenario 3	Scenario 4
19	Improve traveler information on MNWR website	$0 to $20,000	$ 5,000	1	$ 5,000			X	X	X	X
20	Identify alternate dock space for Monomoy ferries	$40 to $150 per mooring rental per year	$ 150	4	$ 600		Does not include costs associated with obtaining parking spaces near the mooring site or transporting ferry passengers to and from the boats.		X		
						Total Capital		$ 255,400	$1,569,800	$ 339,240	$ 109,400
						Total Additional (annual)		$ 300,000	$ 50,000	$ 5,000	$ 2,000

APPENDIX G.   Intervention Evaluation Matrix

Category	Transportation Intervention	Cost	Level of Difficulty to Implement (Technical / Engineering)	Political Sensitivity	Environmental Constraints / Limitations	Impact on Habitat Protection	Public Approval / Support	Visitation Impact	Implementation Time Frame	FWS Ability to Implement	Partnership Necessary for Implementation	Comments
Bike/Ped	More bike racks at headquarters/visitor contact station	Low	Low	Low	Low	Low/+	Much	None/+	Within FY	High	No	
Bike/Ped	More bike racks downtown	Low	Low	Med	Low	Low/+	Some	None/+	Within FY	Med	Yes/Town	This would be simple to execute with permission from landowner.
Bike/Ped	More bike racks at Lighthouse Beach	Low	Low	Low	Low	Low/+	Much	None/+	Within FY	Med	Yes/NPS	This would be simple to execute with NPS partnership
Bike/Ped	Striped bike lanes (convert signed bike route to striped lanes)	High	High	High	Med	Low/+	Little	Some/+	2 years	Low	Yes/Town/MHD	Would likely require roadway widening and possibly some acquisition of right of way.
Bike/Ped	Striped bike lanes on Morris Island Rd. / Causeway	Med	Med	Med	Med	Low/+	Little	Some/+	2 years	Low	Yes/Town	Sufficient right of way exists, but additional paving would be necessary.
Bike/Ped	Causeway bikeway / multiuse path	Low	Low	Low	Low	Low/+	Some	Some/+	1 year	Med	Yes/Town	Assume that the path would be an accessible "soft surface", such as crushed stone.
Bike/Ped	Crosswalk cones in marked crosswalks	Low	Low	Med	Low	Low/+	Some	None/+	Within FY	Med	Yes/Town/MHD (?)	Cones must meet town design standards as well as MUTCD.
Bike/Ped	Marked crosswalks at Main/Shore, between Lighthouse and Beach	Low	Med	Low	Low	Low/+	Much	None/+	1 year	Med	Yes/Town/MHD (?)	Check existing crosswalk locations.

Appendix G. Intervention Evaluation Matrix

Category	Transportation Intervention	Cost	Level of Difficulty to Implement (Technical / Engineering)	Political Sensitivity	Environmental Constraints / Limitations	Impact on Habitat Protection	Public Approval / Support	Visitation Impact	Implementation Time Frame	FWS Ability to Implement	Partnership Necessary for Implementation	Comments
Bike/Ped	Sidewalk from Lighthouse to Bridge St. parking area	Med	Med	Med	Low	Low/+	Some	Some/+	2 years	Med	Yes/Town	Would need to check if it could use existing and available right of way or if it would require taking some of front lawns for sidewalk space. Expect mixed reaction with public – some strong approval and some strong disapproval.
Bike/Ped	Appropriate sidewalk/crosswalk in any satellite parking	Low	Low	Low	Low	Low/+	Much	None/+	2 years	Med	Yes/Town	Needs to be determined later if/when parking location is identified.
Bike/Ped	Partner w/ bike community to encourage short term bike rental in general, and to MNWR	Low	Low	Low	Low	Low/+	Some	Some/+	Within FY	High	Yes/Town (bike/ped)	Depends on ability to partner with bike community and their interest and ability to implement such a system.
Bike/Ped	Partner w/DCR to add information about Chatham and Monomoy at the CCRT rotary	Low	Low	Low	Low	Low/+	Some	Some/+	Within FY	High	Yes/DCR/ Town (bike/ped)	Depends on willingness of DCR to add information.
Transit	Satellite parking at high school and shuttle to downtown, Lighthouse Beach, and Morris Island	High	Med	Low	Low	Low/+	Much	Some/+	2 years	Med	Yes/Town (schools), NPS, CCRTA, CCC	FWS can apply for funding for the vehicles, but developing the routes and plans for operations and maintenance will be necessary. Ongoing vehicle operations and maintenance is the highest cost.
Transit	Satellite parking at elementary school and shuttle to downtown, Lighthouse Beach, and Morris Island	High	Med	Low	Low	Low/+	Much	Some/+	2 years	Med	Yes/Town (schools), NPS, CCRTA, CCC	FWS can apply for funding for the vehicles, but developing the routes and plans for operations and maintenance will be necessary. Ongoing vehicle operations and maintenance is the highest cost.

Appendix G. Intervention Evaluation Matrix

Monomoy National Wildlife Refuge Alternative Transportation Study

Category	Transportation Intervention	Cost	Level of Difficulty to Implement (Technical / Engineering)	Political Sensitivity	Environmental Constraints / Limitations	Impact on Habitat Protection	Public Approval / Support	Visitation Impact	Implementation Time Frame	FWS Ability to Implement	Partnership Necessary for Implementation	Comments
Transit	Expand H2O service to access Lighthouse Beach	Med	Med	Med	Low	Low/+	Some	Some/+	1 year	Low	Yes/CCRTA, CCC, NPS	FWS could apply for funds for additional vehicles, but would not have other involvement. There may be issues will running buses through downtown Chatham to the beach - schedule time, congested narrow roads, potential public opposition.
Transit	Expand H2O service to access Morris Island	Med	Med	Med	Low	Low/+	Some	Some/+	1 year	Low	Yes/CCRTA, CCC	FWS could apply for funds for additional vehicles, but would not have other involvement. There may be issues will running buses through downtown Chatham to Morris Island - schedule time, congested narrow roads, potential public opposition.
Transit	Develop "Flex-style" service for H2O line, with option to access Lighthouse Beach or Morris Island	Med	Med	Med	Low	Low/+	Some	Some/+	2 years	Low	Yes/CCRTA, CCC, NPS	FWS could apply for funds for additional vehicles, but would not have other involvement. There may be issues will running buses through downtown Chatham to Morris Island - schedule time, congested narrow roads, potential public opposition. Could be technically difficult from a transit perspective because Morris Island is so far from other destinations.
Transit	Partner with Chatham Bars Inn to allow others to ride trolley/car to Lighthouse Beach or VC	Low	Low	Med	Low	Low/+	Some	Some/+	Within FY	Low	Yes/Chatham Bars Inn	CBI has not shown any interest in such a partnership

Appendix G. Intervention Evaluation Matrix

Monomoy National Wildlife Refuge Alternative Transportation Study

Category	Transportation Intervention	Cost	Level of Difficulty to Implement (Technical / Engineering)	Political Sensitivity	Environmental Constraints / Limitations	Impact on Habitat Protection	Public Approval / Support	Visitation Impact	Implementation Time Frame	FWS Ability to Implement	Partnership Necessary for Implementation	Comments
Transit	Promote connections to Provincetown and Hyannis for broader Cape-wide transit, and "car-free" visits to Chatham	Low	Low	Low	Low	Med/+	Some	Some/+	1 year	Low	Yes/CCRTA, CCC, NPS, Chambers of Commerce, etc.	This is a priority of CCC, NPS, and other groups, but would primarily not be an implementation activity of FWS. FWS could lend support by providing information on the website, etc.
Transit	Develop water taxi service from Oyster Pond to MNWR	High	High	Med	Med	Low/-	Some	Some/+	5 years	Low	Yes/Town (harbor master)	While the boat could land at Stage Harbor, or at the visitor contact station, neither would be feasible due to ADA and time constraints.
Parking	Provide satellite parking (with shuttle service) for MNWR and Lighthouse Beach at the Chatham High School	Low	Low	Low	Low	Low/+	Much	Some/+	2 years	Med	Yes/Town (schools), NPS, CCRTA, CCC	This relates to the parking component and not the shuttle component
Parking	Provide satellite parking (with shuttle service) for MNWR and Lighthouse Beach at the Chatham Elementary School	Low	Low	Low	Low	Low/+	Much	Some/+	2 years	Med	Yes/Town (schools), NPS, CCRTA, CCC	This relates to the parking component and not the shuttle component
Parking	Widen the Causeway shoulder to provide more space for parking (don't pave, just move fencing)	Med	Med	Med	Med	Low/+	Some	Some/+	1 year	Low	Yes/Town	The Causeway is owned by the Town. The fencing is likely to need to be replaced in the coming years anyway; perhaps FWS could contribute some funds to the effort if the fencing would be moved over.
Parking	Charge for parking at Morris Island	Low	Low	Low	Low	Low/+	Little	Some/-	1 year	High	No	FWS can implement fee through one of several methods

Appendix G. Intervention Evaluation Matrix

Monomoy National Wildlife Refuge Alternative Transportation Study

Category	Transportation Intervention	Cost	Level of Difficulty to Implement (Technical / Engineering)	Political Sensitivity	Environmental Constraints / Limitations	Impact on Habitat Protection	Public Approval / Support	Visitation Impact	Implementation Time Frame	FWS Ability to Implement	Partnership Necessary for Implementation	Comments
Parking	Develop and enforce parking time restrictions at Morris Island	Low	Low	Med	Low	Low/+	Little	Some/-	1 year	High	No	Dependent on FWS's enforcement mechanism/ hiring a law enforcement officer
Parking	Identify satellite parking downtown and provide shuttle for MNWR and Lighthouse Beach	High	High	High	Low	Low/+	Some	Some/+	2 years	Med	Yes/Town, NPS	The Town's position is that parking downtown is so tight already that the lots are not available for MNWR satellite parking. They may be interested in seeking additional satellite parking to relieve downtown pressure.
Parking	Consider diagonal parking on one side of causeway	High	High	Med	Low	Low/+	Little	Some/+	2 years	Low	Yes/Town	Might provide space for more cars to park on the Causeway, but could be problematic in terms of available width for parking and two-way traffic. Causeway is owned by the Town and FWS would be able to do little to support this intervention.
Parking	Build parking deck downtown to provide satellite parking for MNWR and additional parking for Chatham	High	High	High	Med	Low/+	Some	Some/+	> 2 years	Low	Yes/Town	Parking decks are very expensive and might be technically complicated due to ground stability issues and ability to accommodate the weight of the deck and multiple levels of vehicles. Demand for MNWR visitation and parking likely does not warrant this expense and it might be difficult for FWS to justify building new parking rather than utilizing already disturbed land.
Signage/ Traveler Info	Variable message sign at new intersection of Main St, Crowell, Queen Anne Rd, etc.	Med	Med	High	Low	Low/+	Some	Some/+	2 years	Med	Yes/Town, CCC, MHD, volunteers	Could be costly for capital and/or labor. Unclear who would manage the system and to where visitors would be rerouted. Could be packaged with other satellite parking interventions.

Prepared by the U.S. DOT Volpe Center   147

Appendix G. Intervention Evaluation Matrix

Monomoy National Wildlife Refuge Alternative Transportation Study

Category	Transportation Intervention	Cost	Level of Difficulty to Implement (Technical / Engineering)	Political Sensitivity	Environmental Constraints / Limitations	Impact on Habitat Protection	Public Approval / Support	Visitation Impact	Implementation Time Frame	FWS Ability to Implement	Partnership Necessary for Implementation	Comments
Signage/ Traveler Info	Improved directional signage to refuge	Med	Low	Med	Low	Low/+	Some	Much/+	1-2 years	Med	Yes/Town, NPS, MHD?	Would need to work with Town design commission/historical commission, etc. to be ensure that the designs meet design standards, most likely also with FWS HQ, and possibly MHD, depending on where the signs would be located
Signage/ Traveler Info	Informational signage and access information at "satellite" refuge visitor contact downtown	Low	Low	Low	Low	Low/+	Some	Much/+	1 year	High	No	Easy to implement - assuming that FWS is able to identify and acquire a location for a satellite VC
Signage/ Traveler Info	Shuttle featuring interpretive tour	High	Med	Med	Low	Low/+	Some	Much/+	2 years	High	No	Need to acquire vehicle, plan tour, identify who will provide interpretation; needs to couple with alternate parking locations, make plan for vehicle maintenance and operations
Signage/ Traveler Info	Traffic camera at north end of causeway with feed to headquarters/visitor contact station to identify potential congestion/parking issues and facilitate dynamic solutions.	High	Med	Med	Low	Low/+	Some	None/+	2 years	High	Yes/Town, CCC, MHD?	Unclear who would be monitoring the cameras and what solutions they would be able to employ. Needs to couple with other interventions.

Category	Transportation Intervention	Cost	Level of Difficulty to Implement (Technical / Engineering)	Political Sensitivity	Environmental Constraints / Limitations	Impact on Habitat Protection	Public Approval / Support	Visitation Impact	Implementation Time Frame	FWS Ability to Implement	Partnership Necessary for Implementation	Comments
Engineering / roadway infrastructure	Roundabout at intersection of Morris Island, Tisquantum, and Stage Island Road with traveler information on parking availability, weather, etc.	High	High	High	Med/High	Low/-	None	Some/+	5 years	Low	Yes/Town, CCC, MHD?	Could be beneficial in terms of reducing visitor confusion and travel into Quitnesset, but would be expensive and complicated and provide valuable information at a late juncture - after visitors have traveled all the way through Chatham to the VC
Engineering / roadway infrastructure	Additional lane on causeway with reversible direction (two lanes in/one lane out during peak AM hours, two lanes out/one lane in during PM hours)	High	High	High	Med	Low/-	None	Some/+	5 years	Low	Yes/Town, CCC, MHD?	Would require additional paving, which is not desired by Town. Unclear hat traffic to Morris Island really behaves on an AM/PM peak schedule, also unclear what would happen with parking lane
Engineering / roadway infrastructure	Create roundabout with vehicle "drop off" area at intersection of Morris Island, Tisquantum, and Stage Island Road for beach/VC access	High	High	High	Med/High	Low/-	Unknown	Some/+	5 years	Low	Yes/Town, CCC, MHD?	Could be beneficial in terms of reducing visitor confusion and travel into Quitnesset, but would be expensive and complicated. Available land is extremely limited, and the project would require complex planning and design.

Appendix G. Intervention Evaluation Matrix

Monomoy National Wildlife Refuge Alternative Transportation Study

Category	Transportation Intervention	Cost	Level of Difficulty to Implement (Technical / Engineering)	Political Sensitivity	Environmental Constraints / Limitations	Impact on Habitat Protection	Public Approval / Support	Visitation Impact	Implementation Time Frame	FWS Ability to Implement	Partnership Necessary for Implementation	Comments
Engineering / roadway Infrastructure	Relocate most visitor contact station functions to alternate site close to downtown Chatham.	High	High	Med	Low	Low/+	Much	Much/+	5+ years	High	No	Depends on ability to identify and afford space at a suitable location. Would be useful in providing basic information and education to most visitors, and guide those interested in more, to Morris Islands or the Monomoy Islands
Engineering / roadway Infrastructure	Sell oversand vehicle (OSV) permits to cars and trucks seeking access to Monomoy / Morris Island.	Low	High	High	High	High	Unknown					Opportunity for vehicles to directly access certain portions of the Refuge could increase visitation, but no studies have documented demand for OSV permits.
Marine transportation	Identify additional dock space in Chatham for MNWR-related activities	High	Med	Med	Low	Low/+	Some	Much/+	2 - 5 years	Med	Yes/ Town (Landing Officer)	Some technical difficulty and political sensitivity associated with the general shortage of dock space in Chatham.

APPENDIX H.   Additional Bicycle Rack Information

There are a variety of styles of commercial sidewalk bicycle racks, which range in size, cost, capacity, and visual design. Racks that allow for two points of contact (wheel and frame) allow stability to prevent the bicycle from falling over, and they also are more secure in preventing theft. Many of the standard rack styles can be customized to include a logo or other design; an entirely custom design is also possible.

Some of the most common types of racks are shown below (images from Dero Bike Racks http://www.dero.com/).

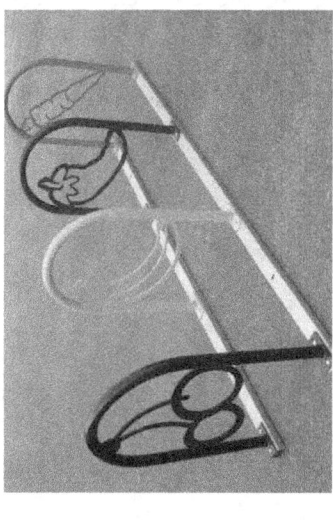

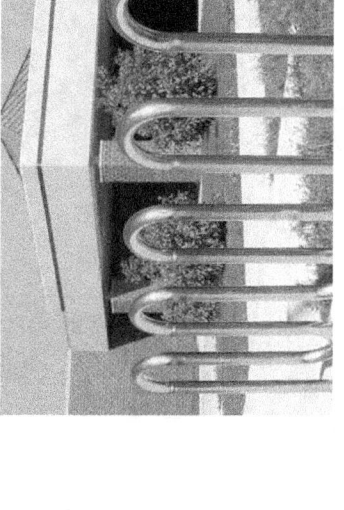

Hitch Rack
Good for use on a sidewalk or other narrow spaces. Design can be customized.

Capacity: 2 bicycles – one on each side.

Cost: ~ $200 per rack

Hoop Rack
Common, secure.
Design can be customized

Capacity: 2 bicycles – one on each side.

Cost: ~$200 per rack

Rolling Rack
Good for a location that has multiple bicycles.

Capacity: 5 to 11 bicycles, depending on number of loops.

Cost: ~$400-700, depending on number of loops

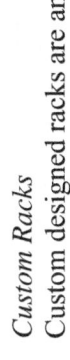

(deer, sunflower, fish)

Campus Rack
Good for a location that has multiple bicycles.

Capacity: 3 to 11 bicycles, depending on number of loops.

Cost: ~$450-900, depending on number of bicycles

"Bicycle" Rack
Fun, artistic bicycle rack.

Capacity: 2 to 4 bicycles.

Cost: ~$400 per rack

Custom Racks
Custom designed racks are an option for a more creative, artistic bicycle parking experience. A rack could be designed with a FWS theme.

Custom racks that are based on an existing hoop or hitch design are likely to be the most cost-effective.

APPENDIX I.   Water Taxi Evaluation

One possibility for providing alternative access to MNWR would be to operate a water taxi from a more centralized location, such as downtown Chatham. The water taxi could depart from a public mooring on Oyster Pond in Chatham, MA; Oyster Pond is roughly a 0.4 mile walk from downtown Chatham, making it accessible to other popular Chatham destinations. The taxi service as discussed below would bring visitors to the MNWR headquarters/visitor contact station on Morris Island, where they would engage in the activities at the station or board the ferry to visit the Monomoy Islands.

The water taxi would travel from a mooring at Oyster Pond, and down the Oyster River to Stage Harbor. From this point the taxi service could take one of two distinct routes:

Route 1: Travel across Stage Harbor and dock at an MNWR owned property on Stage Harbor. From this site, travelers would be required to walk or be shuttled from the MNWR property to the Morris Island headquarters/visitor contact station to access the refuge.
Total approximate water route distance – 3 miles
Total approximate route distance – 3.5 miles

Route 2: Travel out of Stage Harbor, and around both Monomoy Islands. Dock at the existing MNWR headquarters/visitor contact station. Total approximate route distance: 24 miles

Evaluation

There are several limitations to using a water taxi as an alternate form of transportation to bring visitors to MNWR. These issues involve travel through the Oyster River and Stage Harbor, vessel storage, and accessibility issues at the docking points. The main issues are discussed in more detail below.

Travel Time
There are seasonal speed limits of five miles per hour in Oyster Pond, the Oyster River and Stage Harbor, from June 15 – September 15; the entire area is also a no wake zone during that same time period. Due to these restrictions, the trip from an Oyster Pond mooring through Stage Harbor would take at least 30 to 45 minutes, not including boarding and disembarking time. Speed around the Monomoy Islands would be varied due to weather and sea conditions.

Landside Needs
Landside needs for this water taxi include storage during the offseason, ground access to the vessel, as well as maintenance and fueling facilities. These could be difficult or costly to accommodate.

Accessibility
Compliance with the Americans with Disabilities Act (ADA) dictates requirements related both to the vessel and to the locations passengers board and disembark the water taxi. Although the access point at Oyster Pond is likely not fully ADA compliant, it may provide some access opportunities for people with disabilities. However, the arrival points for both Routes 1 and 2, present significant accessibility challenges. The arrival points at Stage Harbor and at the MNWR headquarters/visitor contact station do not have proper docking facilities, or infrastructure for traveling from the boat to the MNWR headquarters/visitor contact station. Further, both sites would require visitors to walk up either a steep incline (Route 1) or steep stairs (Route 2) as part of the access from the boat to the headquarters/visitor

contact station. Both sites would require significant investments in structural and infrastructure improvements to make it so[33]. These improvements would be required for projects using Federal funds.

Navigation

Route 2 involves more complex navigational issues. The water taxi vessel would need to navigate out of Stage Harbor (through a dredged channel) and around the Monomoy Islands. There are many shoals and shifting sand bars in the area. The NOAA Coast Pilot recommends that small vessels with local knowledge can use the area, but that outsiders should avoid the area. Further, the service might not be able to operate on days with poor weather or sea conditions.

Cost

The vessel required for the water taxi service would likely cost upwards of $100,000; ADA compliant facilities including a slip, path and ramp or lift could cost into the millions of dollars. Based upon the fees charged by other similar ferry services, and the Monomoy Island ferry services, FWS could probably reasonably charge between $15 and $20 per ticket for Route 2, if it was reconfigured to serve more as a ferry service, bringing visitors to the Monomoy Islands. For the less scenic Route 1, it would probably not be reasonable to charge more than approximately $5 per ticket. While additional analysis is necessary to determine the cost of operations and maintenance, it is unlikely that ticket revenues would be able to sustain the service financially. Route 1 might also require a van or other vehicle to shuttle passengers from the boat to the visitor contact station.

Conclusions

Due to the limitations posed by the water taxi routes, this intervention does not appear to be feasible as a transportation option. The travel time, lack of ADA compliance and navigation difficulties create a costly and long ride.

While Route 1 has a shorter travel time, there would be sensitivities associated with requiring visitors to walk or be shuttled through the private neighborhood, and might require additional easements over private property. It may be worthwhile to further explore Route 2 as an option to provide a more interpretive, recreational experience; such a service falls beyond the scope of this alternative transportation study.

It should be noted that originating at Oyster Pond is not the only option for a water-based transit service to MNWR; however it was in the only one explored in this section. Oyster Pond was selected for its proximity to downtown Chatham. In the future FWS may wish to consider additional start locations for a water taxi, including Chatham's ocean-side harbors. Utilizing these harbors may reduce some of the challenges associated with a water taxi; however, FWS would still have issues pertaining to cost, time, distance and accessibility.

---

[33] ADA access requirements can be found at: http://www.access-board.gov/adaag/html/adaag.htm

APPENDIX J. Low-Environmental Impact Vehicle Options

Concurrently with the Monomoy National Wildlife Refuge Alternative Transportation Study, the U.S Fish and Wildlife Service engaged the Volpe Center to conduct research on alternative fuel vehicle options for Refuges and public lands throughout the U.S. The research project featured a market assessment and technology assessment. The purpose of the technology assessment was to determine the availability of low-environmental impact vehicles, namely tram and tram-like vehicles, and the feasibility of using those vehicles or their components in the Federal lands operating environment.

The feasibility of vehicles for use within the Federal lands environment was based on an analysis of the typical operating environments (e.g. the road network, geography, topography, and climate in each Region) and on the following stated vehicle characteristics:

a. Can be driven at slower speeds
b. Can be driven on unpaved surfaces including dirt, gravel, sand, and other surfaces
c. Can pull significant loads
d. Have little to no noise impact
e. Have reasonably high depletion time to recharge ratio
f. Feature an ultra-low floor and are ADA-accessible
g. Allow for interpretive tours
h. Can operate in a wide range of temperature
i. Can travel down narrow paths

Based on the vehicle characteristic requirements the Volpe Center identified four market-ready tram vehicles that meet most of FWS's requirements, two proposed tram vehicles, and one manufacturer that has the ability to develop trams to meet FWS needs:

Market Ready Vehicles:
- GatorMoto – Electric Transport Buddy
- Specialty Vehicles – Star II Shuttle
- Trams International - Model 6000
- Maritime Applied Physics Corporation – Electric Tram

Proposed Vehicles:
- Maritime Applied Physics Corporation:
  - Long-Range Electric Tram Design
  - Proposed Hybrid-Electric Tram Design

Tram Vehicle and Part Manufacturers:
- ISE Corporation

An overview of these alternative fuel tram vehicles is provided in the following pages.

GatorMoto
Electro Transport Buddy

Contact Information:
7065 NW 22nd Street, Suite A
Gainesville, FL 32653
1-866-5-GATORS
www.gatormoto.com

Vehicle Characteristics

Speed	Up to 25 mph
Pavement Type	Gravel and dirt; not recommended for beach
Grade	20 percent at full load
Load Carrying Capacity	2500 lb maximum load
Noise	Silent
Range	50 miles (maximum load) per charge (40 miles in below freezing temperatures)
Battery	Trojan Battery – 16 pcs.
Battery Charging	Recharge in approximately 6 hours. Can be plugged into a standard wall socket
Passenger Capacity	Available in 12 and 15 passenger sizes
Requires a CDL to operate	No
ADA-accessible	Yes
Allows for Interpretive Tours	Yes, open air design and 4 speakers fixed on roof
Operable Temperature	Can operate in any climate. Decreased performance if operated in below freezing temperatures
Width of Vehicle	5 feet
Turning Radius	18 feet
Street Legality	All vehicles larger than six passengers can be ordered with everything required for street legal status; however they require special permission from the local authorities to use the vehicle on a public road due to this weight limit.
Cost	$17,995

Specialty Vehicles
Star II Shuttle

Contact Information:
440 Mark Leany Drive
Henderson, NV 89011
1-800-SVI-TRAM
www.specialtyvehicles.com/index.html

Vehicle Characteristics

Speed	22-28 mph
Pavement Type	Pavement, gravel, dirt and sand; however, for better traction it is best if surface is dry and compacted. Loose dirt can get stuck in the brakes and may result in more frequent maintenance.
Grade	Up to 20 percent at full load
Load Carrying Capacity	Up to 2405 lbs
Noise	Very minimal from motor
Range	40-62 miles fully loaded
Battery	Trojan Batteries, 48V or 72V.
Battery Charging	Recharge in 6-8 hours. On board charger option for charging between tours and a stationary standard battery recharge for overnight charging.
Passenger Capacity	Available in 8, 11 and 14-passenger sizes
Requires a CDL to operate	No
ADA-accessible	Yes
Allows for Interpretive Tours	Yes, PA plug-in with microphone and 4 speakers
Operable Temperature	Operates well in most weather conditions, including snow (chains required)
Width of Vehicle	6.3 feet
Turning Radius	15' (8 passenger); 16 (11 passenger) 18' (14 passenger)
Street Legality	The smaller two, 8 and 11-passenger, are able to be licensed as low speed vehicles (LSV). The larger model is too heavy to meet the LSV DMV weight requirements for any type of licensing.
Cost	$14,000; $17,000; $20,000
Other	Battery, motor and controller are accessible under seat

**Trams International
Model 6000E**

Contact Information:
6801 Suva Street
Bell Gardens, CA 90201
562-231-1770
www.tramfactory.com

Vehicle Characteristics

Speed	15 mph
Pavement Type	Available with tire tread and rubber compounds to meet the rigors and demands of different road surfaces including sand, gravel and dirt.
Grade	6-12 percent
Load Carrying Capacity	46 passengers (Rated by passenger capacity not pounds)
Noise	Very minimal
Range	20-25 miles per charge fully loaded
Battery	Lead-acid batteries, Hawker Genesis G12V42AH10EP
Battery Charging	Full recharge in 8 hours (achieve 95 percent state of recharge in less than one hour using conventional constant-voltage charging techniques)
Passenger Capacity	14-18 passengers (plus 28 passenger trailers)
Requires a CDL to operate	Yes, for vehicles that carry 16+ passengers
ADA-accessible	Yes, self storing slide out ramp
Allows for Interpretive Tours	Yes, see-thru roof and PA system with microphone
Operable Temperature	45-115°F
Width of Vehicle	6.9 feet
Turning Radius	25.7 feet
Other	Service friendly – good accessibility to engine (less than 5 minutes to open up completely). Because of limited energy storage it's very important that the venue's drivers and maintenance people be thoroughly and properly trained on site by TI's field service staff.

** The model 6000 is also available in diesel (biodiesel B-20 ready) and propane powered versions

Maritime Applied Physics Corporation (MAPC)
Existing Patuxent Refuge Electric Tram

Contact Information:
1850 Frankfurst Avenue
Baltimore, MD 21226
443-524-3330
http://www.mapcorp.com/

Speed	19 mph
Pavement Type	Unpaved surfaces, such as dirt, gravel and sand, but with durability penalties.
Grade	18 percent
Load Carrying Capacity	20,000 lbs (power car plus trailer)
Noise	Absolutely minimal
Range	21 miles, fully loaded
Battery	Flooded lead-acid deep cycle with water leveling system
Battery Charging	9 hours maximum
Passenger Capacity	17 plus 28 passenger trailer
Requires a CDL to operate	Yes, if more than 16 passengers
ADA-accessible	Yes
Allows for Interpretive Tours	Yes
Operable Temperature	35°F +
Width of Vehicle	80"
Turning Radius	27 feet
Street Legality	No, low speed vehicle
Cost	Unknown – old design. For scale the relative drive train and battery would cost approximately $4,000.

Maritime Applied Physics Corporation (MAPC)
Long-Range Electric Tram Design

Contact Information:
1850 Frankfurst Avenue
Baltimore, MD 21226
443-524-3330
http://www.mapcorp.com/

MAPC has been in discussions with one tram manufacturer about adding its drive train and battery systems to their tram chassis. These discussions focused on the desire to produce a large 50 mile range at minimal cost. MAPC performed an analysis and settled on some components to include in their tram chassis that they believe optimized the design for these goals.

The proposed vehicle has the following characteristics:

Speed	15 mph
Pavement Type	Unpaved surfaces, such as dirt, gravel and sand, but with durability penalties. (Uses standard tram chassis and body).
Grade	20 percent
Load Carrying Capacity	22,000 lbs (power car plus trailer)
Noise	Absolutely minimal
Range	48 miles, fully loaded
Battery	Sealed Absorbed Glass Mat
Battery Charging	4 hours maximum
Passenger Capacity	17 plus 28 passenger trailer
Requires a CDL to operate	Yes, if more than 16 passengers
ADA-accessible	Yes
Allows for Interpretive Tours	Yes
Operable Temperature	30°F +
Width of Vehicle	80"
Turning Radius	27 feet
Street Legality	No, low speed vehicle
Cost	Unknown – not yet built. For scale the relative drive train and battery would cost approximately $14,000.

Maritime Applied Physics Corporation (MAPC)
Proposed Hybrid-Electric Tram Design

Contact Information:
1850 Frankfurst Avenue
Baltimore, MD 21226
443-524-3330
http://www.mapcorp.com/

MAPC is developing a new hybrid-electric tram vehicle. The
proposed hybrid vehicle would have an electric-drive range similar to the Patuxent vehicle, but allow the
generator to be used to operate the vehicle at any time, and/or recharge the battery. This would also allow
the vehicles electric-only range to be more fully utilized. In addition, the chassis would be modified to
perform better on unimproved roads- modified steering geometry to prevent road surface wear, modified
spring rates, improved materials, and efficiently-electrified support systems (power steering, power
brakes) that would enhance durability in the outdoor environment and maximize vehicle range.

The proposed hybrid-electric tram has the following characteristics:

Speed	15 mph
Pavement Type	Custom engineered for off-road use at parks, refuges, and gardens
Grade	20 percent
Load Carrying Capacity	20,000 lbs (power car plus trailer)
Noise	Some: generator can be started at times when impact is noncritical
Range	17 miles on battery only; 75 miles with generator operation also
Battery	Sealed Absorbed Glass Mat
Battery Charging	2 hours maximum
Passenger Capacity	17 plus 28 passenger trailer
Requires a CDL to operate	Yes, if more than 16 passengers
ADA-accessible	Yes
Allows for Interpretive Tours	Yes
Operable Temperature	20°F +
Width of Vehicle	80"
Turning Radius	22 feet
Street Legality	No, low speed vehicle
Cost	Unknown – not yet built. For scale the relative drive train and battery would cost approximately $7,000.
Other	Meets Federal Lands Highway Program § 3021 *Alternative Transportation in Parks and Public Lands* requirements for clean fuel technologies.

ISE Corporation
ThunderVolt Electric Drive System

Contact Information:
12302 Kerran Street
Poway, CA 92064
858-413-1720
www.isecorp.com

ISE Corporation designs and installs the ThunderVolt, an all electric drive system that is ideal for carrying people relatively short distances in off-road environments. ISE works closely with tram chassis manufacturers and, together, develop vehicles to meet their customer's specific needs.

An example of a vehicle ISE has developed using the ThunderVolt system has the following characteristics:

Speed	15 mph (towing)
Grade	Maximum starting grade of 15%; maximum continuous grade 10%
Load Carrying Capacity	Up to 2 trailers
Noise	Very minimal
Range	80 miles per charge
Battery	Zebra NiNaCl
Battery Charging	85% in 3 hours; 100% in 6 hours
Passenger Capacity	Up to 74 (with trailers)
Requires a CDL to operate	Yes, if more than 16 passengers
ADA-accessible	Yes
Allows for Interpretive Tours	Yes
Width of Vehicle	6.7 feet

APPENDIX K. Targeted Stakeholder Meeting

Monomoy National Wildlife Refuge Alternative Transportation Study
Stakeholder Meeting
Chatham Community Center, Club Room
December 18, 2009, 10:30 am – 12:00 pm
Meeting Notes

Participants:
- Carl Melberg, U.S. Fish and Wildlife Service (FWS) Eastern Massachusetts National Wildlife Refuge Complex
- Terry Whalen, Town of Chatham Planning Department
- Clay Schofield, Cape Cod Commission
- Jeff Colby, Town of Chatham Department of Public Works
- Lisa Franz, Chatham Chamber of Commerce
- Anna Biton, U.S. DOT Volpe Center
- Julianne Schwarzer, U.S. DOT Volpe Center

Carl Melberg, the Refuge Planner for the U.S. Fish and Wildlife Service (FWS) Eastern Massachusetts National Wildlife Refuge Complex provided an introduction to the meeting:
- The new Monomoy National Wildlife Refuge (MNWR) refuge manager will be starting January 4th, 2009.
- Mr. Melberg will be overseeing the MNWR Comprehensive Conservation Plan (CCP).
- A FWS solicitor will be coming to determine the boundaries of MNWR.

Anna Biton, a Community Planner leading the alternative transportation study at the John A. Volpe National Transportation Systems Center gave a brief presentation about the study and the goals of the meeting:
- The purpose of this meeting is to begin a dialogue to identify partnership opportunities and to discuss potential transportation alternatives for Chatham.
- One major component of the alternative transportation study was to determine the feasibility and usefulness of alternative transportation to MNWR.

The following information documents the conversations throughout the course of the meeting. The main points have been organized by topic for ease of understanding.

Comprehensive Conservation Plan (CCP)
- The CCP will be an Environmental Impact Statement (EIS)
- The draft CCP will be released for public comment by September 2010; the CCP is scheduled to be finalized by September 30, 2011.
- This alternative transportation study will be an appendix the CCP, and certain aspects will be incorporated into the CCP alternatives section as appropriate.
- Parts of the alternative transportation plan will also serve as objectives in the CCP– helping to shape the best strategy for moving forward.

- By adding these strategies to the CCP, each strategy will have already been vetted or eliminated as a result of the EIS process.

Planning
- Alternatives described in the alternative transportation study to be funded through Federal sources should be included in the Regional Transportation Plan (RTP).
- There will be a 2011 update to the RTP, in which FWS could include projects.

Potential Shuttle
- A summer shuttle/loop was agreed upon by the meeting group as an attractive idea.
- The potential shuttle route could run between the high school and Morris Island.
- A shuttle could serve the beach, downtown businesses and Main Street attractions.
- A shuttle might reduce the traffic congestion on Main Street.
- A partnership with the business community would be critical to the success of the shuttle.
- "Park and ride" originating from downtown lots would be difficult as there is already a great deal of downtown parking pressure.
- The key to a shuttle's success is that it runs frequently and is dependable.
- Due to the many lodging options within walking distance of the proposed shuttle route, a shuttle might increase visitation to MNWR.
- Presently parking right at South Beach is limited to 30 minutes, which could provide some incentive to take the shuttle.
- FWS could bring tour groups, via shuttle to MNWR and increase the awareness of natural resources, but FWS would need to educate tour operators as to where to go and what to do.
- Though the shuttle could serve already parked visitors, signage would also be needed to divert drivers to satellite parking.
- Vehicle operation, maintenance, and housing are important considerations for the shuttle.
- It is possible that FWS and the Town of Chatham could form a partnership to maintain and store the vehicle if FWS were able to purchase the vehicle.
- Any shuttle vehicle would need to be relatively small and preferably have an alternative energy component.
- It would be ideal to coordinate a new shuttle with existing regional service, to provide transfer points.

Parking
- Chatham can provide FWS and Volpe with a report on the Paid Sticker Program, although it did not yield any strong conclusions about the effectiveness of the program as 2009 had many deterrents to using the beach, including bad weather and shark warnings which closed the beach.
- Chatham has been trying to improve shoulder parking on Bridge Street by clearing vegetation, adjusting the grade, and putting up signage.
- Parking is very limited downtown.
- A parking deck could alleviate some parking congestion but is expensive and would be very controversial.

Marine Transport

- An alternate dock location for the ferry service to the Monomoy Islands could potentially catch people earlier in their travels and alleviate some traffic concerns.
- Ryder's Cove and the Fish Pier are logical departure points, but both are very congested.
- An alternate departure point might work better than Morris Island for people visiting the Monomoy Islands.
- A shuttle stopping at new ferry departure points could alleviate some roadway congestion.

Downtown Visitor Contact Station

- An informational downtown visitor contact station with maps and points of discussion for a self guided tour of MNWR would be helpful.
- Better information can help potential visitors know about MNWR and that it is located in in Chatham.
- A downtown visitor contact station might allow visitors to experience part of the MNWR without traveling to Morris Island.
- A downtown visitor contact station could be a leased storefront on Main Street, or could be constructed on a larger lot.
- If a bigger facility were available downtown, it could be possible for MNWR and the Chamber of Commerce to have a joint space.
- A Friends of Monomoy Group could establish a storefront and sell books and small souvenirs.
- The storefront is an appealing option, but would not provide a meeting space.
- MNWR would not want to compete with existing business, however the Chamber of Commerce agreed that this type of shop would be unique, and could be a draw for visitors.

Public Works/Engineering

- Chatham is planning to relocate and reinstall the Causeway fencing – it is listed in their mid-range capital plan and has not been funded to date. This is one of many projects that needs funding and may not be a top priority for the Town.
- Creating a multi-use path on the Causeway has not been considered by the Town, but could be desirable. The Causeway has not been a high priority location for the Bikeways Committee.
- There may be opportunities for FWS to apply for Federal Lands grants that could fund some of these projects, however, the Town may need to take on the maintenance.
- The Town has plans to construct a sidewalk between the Bridge Street and South Beach Parking areas, but is not sure when this project will be completed. An engineer is already engaged in an initial examination of the area between Stage Harbor and the Lighthouse.
- The process for determining public infrastructure projects in Chatham includes: developing a concept and cost estimate, presenting the concept to the public, having the public vet the project, then determining if there are funds available.
- If the public demands a large project, the Town can apply for Federal funding or present the issue at a town meeting to obtain additional funding authorization.
- There is a lot of sensitivity in Chatham towards old structures; the public often wants specific features preserved or restored.

- The Town is presently working with the State to get the sidewalk replaced along Route 28 as part of the planned resurfacing project; Chatham proposed adding curbing and sidewalk, especially north of the rotary.
- In January 2010, there will be a public meeting to discuss the redesign of the intersection at Main Street and Crowell Road. Signage improvements at this intersection will be critical.

Signage/ Kiosks
- Chatham has a traffic study committee that examines signage issues.
- Chatham is not interested in making new redundant signs.
- The Town would need to determine whether a new sign would improve a travel situation or if it would lead to "sign pollution".
- In terms of sign design, well-crafted wooden signs are more desirable than metal signs.
- The Bikeways Committee may agree that more signage is needed in Chatham.
- In the past few years the Town has begun to install information kiosks geared toward cyclists. The Town installs the kiosks and provides maps; the Bikeways Committee provides most of the information.
- A good example of a kiosk is at the termini of the bike path. The Community Annex formerly had two kiosks that will be installed along the bike path.
- The goal of the kiosks is to remedy deficiencies in wayfinding.
- The kiosks seem to be very popular with visitors.
- Oyster Pond might be a prime site for a new kiosk.
- MNWR is not currently listed on the maps, though it could be added to the next version of maps.
- The maps usually highlight general locations, but do not outline on-road routes, such as the one to MNWR.
- The Bikeways Committee may consider a partnership with the Chamber of Commerce or specific local businesses to allow advertising and use the revenue to support the information on the kiosk and the maps.
- FWS could add information to the kiosks as they are a Federal agency, though there may be a different arrangement if the kiosks are funded in part through private advertising revenue in the future.

APPENDIX L. Potential Funding Sources

There are a variety of potential funding sources that FWS and its local partners could apply to in order to pursue access (or other) improvements to MNWR. Preliminary information about several potential sources is provided below.

Federal Sources

Paul S. Sarbanes Transit in Parks Program (TRIP)
Congress established the Paul S. Sarbanes Transit in the Parks Program, formerly Alternative Transportation in Parks and Public Lands (ATPPL) Program, to enhance the protection of national parks and federal lands and increase the enjoyment of those visiting them. Administered by the Federal Transit Administration in partnership with the Department of the Interior and the Forest Service, the program funds capital and planning expenses for alternative transportation systems such as shuttle buses and bicycle trails in national parks and public lands. The goals of the program are to conserve natural, historical, and cultural resources; reduce congestion and pollution; improve visitor mobility and accessibility; enhance visitor experience; and ensure access to all, including persons with disabilities. Funds may be used for projects that are located off-site, if there is an obvious connection to how they support access to the unit by alternate transportation. Federal lands units may partner with local governments or other entities in applying for funds.
Funding levels and application dates for FY2010 have not yet been announced.
For more information see: http://www.fta.dot.gov/funding/grants/grants_financing_6106.html

Refuge Roads and Trails Program (FWS)
Refuge Roads are public roads within a unit of the National Wildlife Refuge System for which title and maintenance responsibility is vested in the United States Government. Congress authorized $29 million each year from FY 2005 through FY 2009, of which approximately $25 million is expected to be available for allocation to the FWS. Funds are available for maintenance and improvements on Refuge Roads within the National Wildlife Refuge System. This includes project planning and contract administration as well as construction. Enhancements such as comfort stations, parking lots, bicycle/pedestrian facilities and interpretive signage related to roads are also allowable.
The Federal Lands Highways Division offices are available to assist with applications.
For more information see:
http://www.fws.gov/refuges/roads/road_faqs.html
http://flh.fhwa.dot.gov/

Federal Lands Highways Division (FLH)
The Office of Federal Lands Highway (FLH) provides program stewardship and transportation engineering services for planning, design, construction, and rehabilitation of the highways and bridges that provide access to and through federally owned lands. The primary purpose of the FLHP is to provide financial resources and technical assistance for a coordinated program of public roads that service the transportation needs of Federal and Indian lands.

Discretionary program: The Public Lands Highways – Discretionary (PLHD) Program provides funding for transportation planning, research, and engineering and construction of, highways, roads, parkways, and transit facilities that are within, adjacent to, or provide access to Indian reservations and Federal public lands, including national parks, refuges, forests, recreation areas, and grasslands. PLH funds can be used for any type of Title 23 transportation project providing access to or within Federal or Indian lands and may be used for the State/local matching share for apportioned Federal-aid Highway Funds, as described in 23 USC 120(l). The program is administered by the Federal Highway Administration's Federals Lands Highway Office.

Under 23 U.S.C. 204(h), eligible projects under the PLH program may also include the following:

- Transportation planning for tourism and recreational travel, including the National Forest Scenic Byways Program, Bureau of Land Management Back Country Byways Program, National Trail System Program, and other similar Federal programs that benefit recreational development.
- Adjacent vehicular parking areas.
- Interpretive signage.
- Acquisition of necessary scenic easements and scenic or historic sites.
- Provision for pedestrians and bicycles.
- Construction and reconstruction of roadside rest areas, including sanitary and water facilities.
- Other appropriate public road facilities such as visitor centers as determined by the Secretary.
- A project to build a replacement of the federally owned bridge over the Hoover Dam in the Lake Mead National Recreation Area between Nevada and Arizona.

Transportation Enhancements

Fish and Wildlife Service stations are eligible to apply for Transportation Enhancements (TE) activities. These are funded by the Federal Highway Administration and managed by State Departments of Transportation (DOT). TE projects must be one of 12 eligible activities and must be related to surface transportation. Matching funds are required, but can be in-kind in some cases, and can be Refuge Roads Programs funds or other FWS appropriated money.

The 12 eligible activities include:
- Pedestrian and bicycle facilities
- Pedestrian and bicycle safety and educational activities
- Acquisition of scenic or historic easements and sites
- Scenic or historic highway programs including tourist and welcome centers
- Landscaping and scenic beautification
- Historic preservation
- Rehabilitation and operation of historic transportation buildings, structures or facilities
- Conversion of abandoned railway corridors to trails
- Inventory, control, and removal of outdoor advertising
- Archaeological planning & research
- Environmental mitigation of runoff pollution and provision of wildlife connectivity
- Establishment of transportation museums

For more information see: http://www.enhancements.org/

Community Development Block Grant (CDBG)

The Community Development Block Grant (CDBG) program is a flexible program administered through the U.S. Department of Housing and Urban Development (HUD) that provides communities with resources to address a wide range of unique community development needs. FWS would have to partner with the Town of Chatham to apply for the funds, which could potentially be used toward sidewalk improvements or wayfinding campaigns.

For more information see: http://www.hud.gov/offices/cpd/communitydevelopment/programs/

Other Sources

People-Powered Movement
People-Powered Movement offers startup/capacity building matching grants for organizations seeking to provide alternative transportation options and increase bicycling and walking in a particular setting. The goal of these grants is to leverage private and public investment and launch campaigns that clearly demonstrate an ability to grow and sustain biking and walking organizations. Grants will be used for organizational development, to hire staff, to stimulate membership, and for other organizational tools to foster a sustainable advocacy organization. Successful applicants will demonstrate how these capacity building activities will impact new and existing campaigns and programs to increase biking and walking. Priority for Startup/Capacity Building Grants will be given to organizations serving cities and states that demonstrate the greatest potential for biking and walking advocacy organizations. A "Friends of Monomoy" group, should it be created, might be eligible to apply for funds through this program. For more information see: www.peoplepoweredmovement.org

William P. Wharton Trust
The William P. Wharton Trust provides grant funds to 501(c)(3) organizations engaged in natural areas preservation, primarily in Massachusetts and New England, including funding acquisitions of land for conservation purposes; management techniques designed to improve environmental quality and species diversity; bird and forestry research and management, especially at the applied level rather than the theoretical or molecular level; or creation of materials or projects designed to foster an appreciation of and a concern for wildlife and natural systems.

Transportation projects that improve visitor experience and reduced reliance on single-occupancy vehicle access to MNWR could potentially qualify. A "Friends of Monomoy" group, should it be created, might be eligible to apply for funds through this trust.
For more information see: www.williampwhartontrust.org/

American Canoe Association
The American Canoe Association provides grants for water trail development. Grants are available only to local paddling clubs, but could be relevant for a "Friends of Monomoy" group or other local paddling group to explore the creation of a "water trail", or other water access improvements around Morris Island and the Monomoy Islands.
For more information see:
www.americancanoe.org/site/c.lvIZIkNZJuE/b.4859097/k.DA44/Stewardship_Grants.htm

The Cape Cod Foundation
The Cape Cod Foundation offers grants to non-profit organizations in Barnstable County. The Nonprofit Support Program might be very helpful in starting up a "Friends of Monomoy" group. For more information see: www.capecodfoundation.org

Recreational Equipment, Inc. (REI) Grants
Conservation Grants - grants averaging $5,000 for grassroots organizing and D.C. lobbying to protect lands and waterways, make them more accessible to people who enjoy the outdoors, and better utilize and preserve our natural resources for recreation. Community Recreation Grants - grants of $500 to $5,000 for outdoor programs that increase access, encourage involvement, and promote safety for outdoor muscle-powered sports. Great Places Grants - $15,000 to $25,000 for projects protecting muscle-powered recreation sites.

A "Friends of Monomoy" group, should it be created, might be eligible to apply for funds through this program. For more information see: www.rei.com

Wildlife Habitat Incentive Program (WHIP)
The Wildlife Habitat Incentive Program provides assistance to private landowners with sensitive habitat on their property. Examples of eligible lands in Massachusetts include privately owned grasslands, shrub lands, and young forest, freshwater wetlands, upland oak forest, pitch pine/scrub oak habitat, coastal habitats, and rivers and streams. This program could potentially be of interest and assistance to some neighbors on Morris Island.
For more information see: www.ma.nrcs.usda.gov.

Other Potential Sources of In-Kind Assistance

It may be possible for FWS to coordinate with faculty and students at the following academic institutions to coordinate study programs or receive in-kind assistance with trail planning, signage and wayfinding campaign planning and development, or other planning-related activities:

Conway School of Landscape Design (Conway, MA) www.csld.edu;
UMass-Amherst Department of Landscape Architecture and Regional Planning studios (Amherst, MA) www.umass.edu/larp;
Harvard Graduate School of Design (Cambridge, MA) www.gsd.harvard.edu/;
MIT Department of Urban Studies and Planning http://dusp.mit.edu; and
Wentworth Institute of Technology www.wit.edu

REPORT DOCUMENTATION PAGE

Form Approved
OMB No. 0704-0188

The public reporting burden for this collection of information is estimated to average 1 hour per response, including the time for reviewing instructions, searching existing data sources, gathering and maintaining the data needed, and completing and reviewing the collection of information. Send comments regarding this burden estimate or any other aspect of this collection of information, including suggestions for reducing the burden, to Department of Defense, Washington Headquarters Services, Directorate for Information Operations and Reports (0704-0188), 1215 Jefferson Davis Highway, Suite 1204, Arlington, VA 22202-4302. Respondents should be aware that notwithstanding any other provision of law, no person shall be subject to any penalty for failing to comply with a collection of information if it does not display a currently valid OMB control number.
PLEASE DO NOT RETURN YOUR FORM TO THE ABOVE ADDRESS.

1. REPORT DATE *(DD-MM-YYYY)* May 2010	2. REPORT TYPE Final	3. DATES COVERED *(From - To)* August 2008 - May 2010

4. TITLE AND SUBTITLE Alternative Transportation Study: Monomoy National Wildlife Refuge	5a. CONTRACT NUMBER
	5b. GRANT NUMBER
	5c. PROGRAM ELEMENT NUMBER

6. AUTHOR(S) Anna Biton Theresa Perrone Julianne Schwarzer	5d. PROJECT NUMBER 982108H116 - Monomoy
	5e. TASK NUMBER
	5f. WORK UNIT NUMBER

7. PERFORMING ORGANIZATION NAME(S) AND ADDRESS(ES) The Volpe National Transportation Systems Center U.S. Department of Transprotation 55 Broadway Cambridge, MA 02142	8. PERFORMING ORGANIZATION REPORT NUMBER DOT VNTSC FWS-10-01

9. SPONSORING/MONITORING AGENCY NAME(S) AND ADDRESS(ES) U.S. Fish and Wildlife Service Refuge Roads Program, Washington Office Division of Visitor Services and Communications 4401 N. Fairfax Dr., Room 634 Arlington, VA 22203	10. SPONSOR/MONITOR'S ACRONYM(S)
	11. SPONSOR/MONITOR'S REPORT NUMBER(S)

12. DISTRIBUTION/AVAILABILITY STATEMENT

Public distribution/availability.

13. SUPPLEMENTARY NOTES

14. ABSTRACT

This report provides an overview of the historic and current visitation, infrastructure, and transportation conditions related to Monomoy National Wildlife Refuge and the surrounding areas in Chatham, MA. The study defines transportation-related goals for the refuge and study area, and identifies many potential solutions, grouped into the following categories: Multi-Modal Engineering Improvements; Vehicular Parking Improvements; Transit Service; Signage, Wayfinding, and Information; and Other Visitor Access. These specific potential solutions were then grouped and analyzed as alternative scenarios that could accomplish study goals in a variety of ways. The analysis supports the Monomoy Comprehensive Conservation Plan, which is currently in progress; all NEPA compliance will be conducted as part of the Comprehensive Conservation Plan.

15. SUBJECT TERMS

wildlife refuge; alternative transportation; transportation, visitor experience, shuttle service

16. SECURITY CLASSIFICATION OF:			17. LIMITATION OF ABSTRACT	18. NUMBER OF PAGES	19a. NAME OF RESPONSIBLE PERSON Nathan Caldwell
a. REPORT	b. ABSTRACT	c. THIS PAGE	NA		19b. TELEPHONE NUMBER *(Include area code)* (703) 358-2205
None	None	None			

Reset

Standard Form 298 (Rev. 8/98)
Prescribed by ANSI Std. Z39.18